"Never before have there b _____ ise your
profile and build a reputation. Having _____ e to you
and creates new opportunities. Warren has written an easy to read,
easy to implement guide which is a must read for anyone who wants
to get ahead."

Dr. Ivan Misner, NY Times best-selling author
and Founder of BNI

"This book is a triumph. A thoroughly relevant, engaging and well-
written must read for anyone who wants to win friends and influence people."

Guy Rigby, Head of entrepreneurial services at
Smith and Williamson and author of best-selling
book From Vision to Exit: The Entrepreneur's
Guide to Building and Selling a Business

"When I first met Warren Cass I was instantly struck by his authentic
presence. In *Influence*, he shares his vast reservoirs of practical knowledge and innate wisdom in a way that's easy for the reader to absorb
and apply. If you are struggling to stand out from today's competitive marketplace, this book will enable you to transform your personal
impact and allow your message to reverberate within the hearts and
minds of others. Warren's honest and easy writing style holds the
power to influence your entire life. This book is an absolute must read
if you want to operate at an even higher level to create more of the
results you want in all aspects of your life."

Nikki Owen, Global Thought Leader on Charisma,
Award Winning Speaker and Bestselling Author

"In an age where building a trusted personal brand matters more than
ever before, Warren has created a road map that's packed with ideas
and easy to action. Honestly written and teaches skills that are invalu-
able for life."

Ren Kapur MBE, Founder and CEO, X-Forces

"Warren was the FIRST person I talked to when I set up my business
ten years ago. The fact that he gave me great advice is not the point
here; the fact that he had established himself as an influencer in the
start-up market, all those years ago, is. Social proof is perhaps even
more valid these days than way back then and when Warren talks,

I listen. He is the go-to guy amongst professionals and I am thrilled he is now willing to share his wisdom with a wider audience. If you really want to want to learn from someone who has tasted success and setbacks and now tells you in a relaxed yet concise way all you need to know to increase your social proof . . . read this book"

Bill Morrow, Founder, AngelsDen.com,
named World's Most Influential figure in
Alternative Finance by City AM.

"In a world increasingly focused on artificial intelligence, it is important that we do not lose sight of our emotional intelligence. This book is a must read for anyone who wants to understand their own power of influence to improve the world around them. Every page is thought-provoking with numerous practical applications, even for the most seasoned of influencers. Enjoy the discovery for yourself."

Barnaby Wynter, Communications Director,
Lara Group PLC

"Developing your network and reputation is a must for anyone seeking success in business, who knows you is more important than who you know. In this book, Warren delivers tried and tested techniques that anyone can apply immediately to increase their influence and raise their profile. Essential reading."

Andy Lopata, International Speaker and Author on the subject of
Networking

"At last, a book on influence written post-internet, which contains practical and easy to apply strategies. Whether you just want that promotion or to be a known authority in your field, Warren has created your very own blueprint."

Nigel Risner, Award-Winning Leadership Speaker and Author

"Whilst Warren admits to making mistakes both large and small, his relentless involvement in small business development allows him to have positive influence and to build one of the world's best assets, available to all; his network. Through his well-organised, well-administered and intelligently applied approach, anyone and everyone is capable of placing themselves in the right rooms, with the right people and being brave enough to step outside their comfort zones to introduce themselves to strangers."

Lara Morgan, Entrepreneur, Investor,
Speaker and Author

"What's really clever about Warren's book is that it invites you to be part of the narrative, contextualising all of the lessons so they are relevant to you. By the time you have finished it you will have total clarity on what you need to do to live a more influential life."

Geoff Ramm, Author of Celebrity Service *and* OMG Marketing

"Warren's book is a bang up-to-date exploration of what influence is and how to use the concept to your advantage. It is about using influence respectfully and is free of the old Machiavellian approaches. A must read for anyone trying to get on and make the progress they feel they deserve."

Robert Craven, Author, Grow Your Service Firm

"Influence is one of those things that everybody wants but nobody knows quite what it is or how to get it. The ability to make people take certain actions, think certain thoughts, say certain things and feel certain ways is a fundamental skill for success. And never has influence been a more desirable quality than in today's crazy world of noise, distrust and confusion. Warren Cass is one of the greatest influencers I know, and this superb book is the blueprint for high level connecting, reputation building and influencing."

Rob Brown, Speaker and Author of Build Your Reputation

"This book reflects Warren's approach to life. He understands the first principle of relationship building: 'What's in it for you?' Over the years he has set up so many events to create opportunities for others. Warren's whole attitude is authentically reflected in this book."

Will Kintish, International Speaker and Author on Networking

"Warren Cass is a thought leader for the 21st century who has put together the perfect guide to influencing and persuading others, in business and in life. There's a new kid on the block for Robert Cialdini fans. Drawing on dozens of examples from real life, Warren covers every conceivable topic ranging from what to wear through to positioning on Google and in social media. Read this book if you want to improve your wealth, your relationships or your reputation."

Daniel Barnett, Employment Law Barrister, Outer Temple Chambers

'In this comprehensive book, Warren uncovers how you can build your influence in today's technological world.'

Grant Leboff, CEO of StickyMarketing.com,
International Speaker and Author

"This book is THE manual if you want to be successful in your relationships (business and personal), your communication, marketing, sales, business meetings or any interaction with other people. Warren has written it from a position of years of understanding, study and practice. It explains every single topic you need to improve your influence with others. It also wonderfully explains all of the principles in many ways including much quoted research, practical world-wide examples, statistics and philosophy. This is my 'carry around reference book' to dip into before any important meeting or to help with any business project where I need a competitive edge. It should be yours too."

Andy Gwynn, Business Coach, Entrepreneur, Author
and Professional Speaker.

"Warren is one of a kind and his network, passion to help others and charisma is unrivalled. This book captures the essence of who and what he is about, which makes it practical, real, and easy to implement. There are many strategies to build more influence in your life, and you will struggle to find one not in this book. Warren has comprehensively researched what it means to be influential in a digital age (whilst not forgetting good old fashioned face-to-face persuasion), and written the definitive guide. You will gain so much from reading this, and it's a book that you will re-read and pick up frequently."

Adam Harris, Vistage Chair, Business Coach
and Speaker

"Stunning. A brilliant read that will inspire you to maximise your contacts to the full so opportunity comes to you."

Simon Chapin, CEO Greenstones, Speaker and Author inspiring, challenging and supporting Accountants to be the best they can be.

"If you want to be a more impactful leader and grow your sphere of influence, this insightful no-nonsense book is your step-by-step guide filled with the tools you will need."

Nicola Cook, Speaker, Author and CEO of Company Shortcuts

"I was so engrossed in Warren's book that I read it from cover to cover in one sitting. What really stood out for me were the terrific personal stories he used to make important points, including stories of when he messed up big time in his younger years; I cringed along with him. Some of the tips he gives to help you dig out your own personal stories to share in blog posts and speeches are brilliant. Warren also shares some superb resources to help get top-class PR coverage. This author gives, gives, gives; the mark of a world-class influencer."

Christopher John Payne, Effort-Free Media Ltd,
christopherjohnpayne.com

"A brilliant book written by a brilliant man to help ambitious people create brilliant success. But then, I am biased. . ."

Susan Manen, Warren's Mum and Biggest Fan

INFLUENCE

INFLUENCE

How to Raise Your Profile, Manage Your Reputation and Get Noticed

Warren Cass

WILEY

Library of Congress Cataloging-in-Publication Data is Available:

ISBN 9780857087157 (paperback)

ISBN 9780857087164 (ePDF)

ISBN 9780857087171 (ePub)

Cover Design: Wiley

Set in 11/14, Myriad Pro by SPi Global, Chennai, India

10 9 8 7 6 5 4 3 2 1

MIX

Paper from
responsible sources

FSC   FSC® C013604
www.fsc.org

CONTENTS

ACKNOWLEDGEMENTS

I have learned from so many people over the last 40+ years – by watching how they interact with others, deliver a keynote, control the sales cycle or entice a romantic interest. Most of the time they were unaware of the lessons they were teaching me, or the influence they were having.

This is the benefit of being a student of people, of being fascinated by folk. Every day is quite literally a school day.

My first real memory of learning influence by observation was watching my father when I was a child. My Dad was a military man from the age of 17 and served with the Royal Air Force. He wasn't a particularly high rank or highly decorated, but he was hugely popular and charismatic.

As a child I would watch proudly as my Dad commanded a room, or was life and soul of the party. People responded to him, he held their attention and they always left smiling.

I have often wondered what he could have achieved outside of the military with his very natural ability to influence.

Anyway, I love you Dad and this book is the result of a journey inspired by you.

Over the years I have started several businesses and worked with some amazing people. It didn't always work out, but every interaction helped me learn more about myself and about human nature.

To all of those I have worked with, thank you.

I am profoundly grateful to have such a rich, diverse and supportive network. People with shared values who freely exchange knowledge and ideas.

If you consider yourself part of my network or my friend, then know I appreciate our relationship.

Lastly, I would like to thank my wonderful wife Janet and two beautiful kids Elliott and Jodie, who give me unconditional support every day. **Love you guys!**

Warren Cass

INTRODUCTION

As a 17-year-old lad with only one ambition at the time (to own a nightclub), I took a significant step towards that goal by becoming the assistant manager of the largest nightclub in Southwest England at that time.

You see, getting the role in the first place was as a result of a little influence I had already started to build, albeit unknowingly. As a student I had organised a few large parties, and even turned a profit. This got me known, even beyond my crowd or target audience.

At the time I was studying at college, but I was struggling to concentrate; always distracted by thoughts of getting out into the big wide world and making some money.

This hadn't gone unnoticed. One of my teachers realised I was close to leaving my studies. She knew about my parties and she also knew the owner of the nightclub, so she connected the dots and introduced me.

Sure enough I got the interview and, up against more experienced applicants, got the job. The basic skills of persuasion were already there and I certainly wasn't lacking in confidence.

But alas, it was less than a year later that I learned my first hard lesson: I was fired for being a cocky little shit. I had become overconfident, even arrogant. I had started to believe my own hype (never a good thing). Simply put, I had started rubbing people up the wrong way and wasn't showing them the respect they deserved . . . and this naturally had consequences.

I see now that I was just immature. I was 17 years old with 120 staff working underneath me. I wasn't even old enough to have a drink on the other side of the bar. It had all just gone to my head. Needless to say I was heartbroken. But on reflection it was well deserved. I was devastated and embarrassed and now had to face my family and friends as an unemployed, college dropout.

Overnight I acquired a different reputation. Instead of respect I felt ridicule and, what was worse, it was all self-inflicted. You see, the reason I was fired was because I had become too full of myself. My overconfidence masked a lack of any real leadership skills or experience.

It was a fantastic lesson in humility. And looking back I wouldn't change a single thing about it. You see, in that instant I learned that it REALLY matters how you treat people, and so I vowed never to make that same mistake again.

Looking back at my career since then, I can see clearly that every success I have ever experienced was about my influence, or my ability to influence. Sure, I needed to be able to follow through, deliver on the promise or have a good idea in the first place; but without any influence – even with the best ideas in the world – it is almost impossible to succeed.

WHY READ THIS BOOK?

I hope this is a question you ask yourself before reading any book. Time is precious. In today's society attention is a commodity and the competition to grab it is fierce, even whilst our attention spans continue to shrink and our preference is to consume information in smaller bite-size chunks.

Before I started writing, I had to consider my answer to a similar question: '**Why Write This Book?**'

Over the years, as a public speaker, I have been asked continually, 'Do you have a book?' Influence is a topic I have spoken about for a long time, and whilst my content was useful to my audiences (largely entrepreneurs and small business owners), my public speaking was just a way of raising my profile and that of my business brand.

I didn't want to write for the sake of writing. I value my own time so much that I needed to be really clear on the desired outcome for anyone reading, before I started to type.

So, let me answer the question and then I will justify my answer.

You should read this book if you:

- Want to be more successful.
- Believe your reputation can make or break you, your career or your business.
- Think the path to success is easier with influential friends or contacts.

- Understand social proof is more important today than ever before.
- Believe you would make more progress in life if you improved the quality of your network.
- Know with more influence you would win new clients, get that promotion, attract people to you.

Hopefully, you are still reading. And, if so, here's my promise to you: this is going to be a simple blueprint for anyone that wants to increase awareness of themselves or their brand and genuinely wants to be better at motivating behaviours and outcomes. Because of the way I have written this book, you will spend time reflecting on your own situation/circumstance and start to form your own strategy.

I will not waffle or give you 10 examples of a point where one will do. I respect your time too much. I will not patronise you and assume you know nothing. However, I'll assume you have some common sense and a healthy level of ambition, whatever your situation. After all, you are reading a personal development book.

Just like you (I hope), every day for me is a school day. I am always discovering new things and I want to share with you the simple lessons I have learned, and the observations I have made along the way as an entrepreneur, business owner, friend and student of people.

Over the following chapters, I promise to lay it all out in the hope that you can extract the nuggets you need to take your influence to the next level. If you can implement just one good idea, and it makes a difference for you, I will be pleased. You can always let me know what it is @WarrenCass.

Also, before I go any further, I want to acknowledge that there are several great books on this subject – classics, in fact. I recommend reading them. But I wanted to write this to reflect upon how society has changed, and share why I feel that, to be influential today, you need more weapons in your armoury than simply those around face-to-face communication.

Influence is such a big topic which incorporates so many other aspects of communication (written, body language, NLP etc.), alongside thought leadership, authority, reputation, relationships and trust. The internet only adds another, more complicated, dimension.

The classic example on this topic is *How to Make Friends and Influence People* by Dale Carnegie, which focuses mainly on your interpersonal skills and your persuasive effect on others. Yes, I know it is more than that, but remember: this book was first published in 1937 and society has changed massively since then – with influence becoming a much bigger subject in the digital age.

SO WHY ME?

I am not claiming to rub shoulders with giants or to be on the top 10 rich list. I have enjoyed success though, both as a speaker and as a business owner. I have built an impressive network of people I greatly admire and value, many of whom I am proud to call my friends, and many who have had a profound impact on my outcomes.

Through our online brands we have built and attracted tens of thousands of subscribers and run over 1000 networking events. We have made a ton of mistakes: some minor, and some which cost us dearly. All of them, though, provided lessons and clarity which I will endeavour to share in the pages that follow.

Over the years I have worked with major brands and household names, including Microsoft, Santander, O2, Orange, BlackBerry, Telegraph and Volvo, to name just a few. Earning the credibility to work with such established brands hasn't happened by accident. It is the result of developing an understanding: how to establish a relationship with the appropriate person within an organisation and how to make the right approach.

Lastly, I don't believe everyone wants world domination. You might be reading this because you simply want to generate some more sales, or get that dream job/promotion. Influence is not just reserved for the super successful. We can all become more influential, and in this book I hope to show you how.

MAKING THE MOST OF THIS BOOK

I have written this book in a conversational easy-to-read style. I wanted to ensure that the simple concepts I share are both easy to understand and easy to implement.

There are questions at the end of each chapter which should get you one step closer to action, alongside some practical ideas you can implement straight away.

If you understand the principles, take action. It was the late, great educator Stephen Covey who said 'To know and not to do, is really not to know.' I wish I had really learned that as a younger man.

You will notice that I use quotes throughout the book to share what other great leaders have said on these topics. Read a little further and you may just realise another reason for them.

> *I appreciate that many of you will already be familiar with some of the points I am making. Hell, you may even consider them obvious. That's absolutely fine. My intention is not to patronise. I recognise that people reading this book will have varying degrees of knowledge and experience, so consider these points as useful reminders and move on. But, before you do, ask yourself honestly if you are applying these lessons in practice. If not, do you really know?*

Serendipity is not a strategy. I have always achieved my best results when I have done things on and with purpose, and I encourage you to do the same.

At the end of each chapter, reflect on what you have just read and how it applies to you. What could you change to get better outcomes? Do these new approaches reveal low-hanging fruit you can pluck immediately for some instant results?

It is really important to be totally honest with yourself. There is nothing that irritates more than delusional people, ignorant of how they come across and believing they are brilliant at everything they do. Make sure you are not one of them. Think critically about yourself and consider seeking feedback from those close to you, who you trust to be honest and constructive.

Lastly, thoughts fade and ideas if not recorded can disappear for good. I have left some space for you to reflect and record your thoughts within the book. Please scribble all over it if you think it will encourage a better outcome. Alternatively, you can visit my website InfluenceTheBook.com and download the **Influence Template** for free.

So, let's get started.

INFLUENCE

1

WHAT IS INFLUENCE?

So, what exactly is influence?

Some people influence with the words they use, the ideas they share, the stories they tell and the inspiring actions they take. Others have influence because of the positions they hold, the wealth they have or the company they keep.

There simply is no right or wrong way to influence. Everything is a factor. We are all influenced by people, places, events and situations . . . all of the time!

In a nutshell, influence is about affecting an outcome. It is about motivating a behavioural change or an action. It is about you, and understanding the impact you have on other people and their perceptions of you. It's about progressing things without forcing them or being pushy.

For me, when I imagine someone who is highly influential, a ton of words spring to mind to potentially describe them . . .

Reputation	Authoritative
Charismatic	Leader
Authentic	Humble
Integrity	Confident
Persuasive	Generous
Enthusiastic	Passionate
Knowledgeable	Connected
Communicator	Powerful
Respectful	

Throughout this book these words are going to feature strongly, and there is a summary/exercise chapter at the back designed to help you really reflect on what these words mean to you and, more importantly, how they apply to you.

If you just read this book then I am sure you will find some useful ideas which can help you push forwards. But if you really reflect, and relate the content to yourself, I believe you will get much more, *and* your strategy will become clear.

Imagine a business leader, celebrity or politician, for example. They probably get inundated with requests for media interviews, they are wealthy, maybe they have a best-selling book and speak/ perform on stages across the world to huge audiences.

But is influence really restricted to celebrity? I don't believe you have to be a person of influence to be influential. We all influence behaviours every day, mainly without even knowing it. People change my perspective, my behaviours and my decisions all the time without the faintest idea of the impact they have had on me.

> *'Parents are our children's first heroes! Your influence matters! Wield it wisely with passion and purpose!'*
>
> **Anonymous**

Think about the most influential people in your life. Mum and Dad will be right up there for most people, but it is unlikely that they are captains of industry. Yet their social conditioning from day one has helped you form your values and your moral compass – maybe even your political or religious leanings.

Teachers can have the same profound effect. Most of us, I am sure, can name at least one teacher who really got through to us. Mine was Mr Nesbitt, my English teacher, who understood my disruptive nature and challenged and dared me instead of being authoritarian. He turned learning into a game, which appealed to my competitive nature. As a result he got the best of me compared to every other subject. I doubt Mr Nesbitt remembers who I am, but I shall never forget him. (In the unlikely event you are reading this Sir, thank you, I doff my cap . . . and who knew I would end up writing a book. ;-)

The influence of a good teacher, mentor or boss can never be erased. What mark do you leave on those who look up to you?

Sometimes we are influenced to revolt against the examples we are set. We adopt contrary behaviours based on consequences or our own disapproval of the authority figures in our lives.

Some of the people who have influenced us over the years did so intentionally, but I am sure many will have had no idea of the impact they had or the value they added.

> 'You don't have to be a person of influence to be influential. In fact, the most influential people in my life are probably not even aware of the things they have taught me.'
>
> **Scott Adams**

Many of the things that influence us day to day go completely unnoticed on a conscious level, yet can change our attitudes and behaviour patterns. For example, witnessing and being moved by a simple act of kindness is far more likely to make us more generous in the hours that follow. Or getting caught up in an angry exchange might make us more irritable for the rest of the day.

Human beings are like sponges, emotionally we are affected by the world around us every day. We subconsciously pick up on other people's micro expressions, on advertising messages, and on moods and atmospheres in the world around us. These in turn can have a knock-on effect on others. Which means we are potentially being influenced by people we haven't even met.

Your job requires you to influence people pretty much all of the time. It may be persuading people to advocate for you, creating new relationships, encouraging support or inspiring ideas. Whatever form it takes, the better you are at influencing, the better the results you will achieve.

Our physical state can influence others and even affect our attractiveness. Therefore, by simply managing our physical state we can become more influential.

For example, have you ever been in a crowded room and watched the domino effect as one person yawns and many others follow suit? Or seen someone laughing hysterically and, without knowing why, found yourself laughing along too?

Many studies have concluded that this is because we are empathetic creatures, some of you will have just yawned even imagining a room full of people yawning. I have influenced you right here, right now. ;-) We will cover this in more detail later in the book.

Here's something to think about . . . Every great person, throughout history, has in turn been influenced by others. Influencers are influenced, great leaders have been led and are willing to follow.

For example, Woody Allen was influenced by Hemmingway, Muhammad Ali by Martin Luther King, Tim Burton by Bram Stoker, Jane Austin and Charles Dickens by William Shakespeare, Stephen Fry by Oscar Wilde – the list goes on and on but I am sure you get the point.

So, what does this tell us? It tells us that we all need to be receptive students as well as generous teachers. We need to be open, with a thirst to learn more and be exposed to new ideas.

I have heard people say on many occasions (especially in speaker's circles) that there are no new ideas, just old messages repackaged. Whilst I don't subscribe to this entirely, I do believe all great leaders accept the influence of others, but have the ability and vision to apply their own experiences to what they have learned to evolve ideas, thereby pushing the boundaries and challenging the next generation.

From a business perspective, influence is an essential weapon in your armoury: leaders need to inspire their teams; marketers need to influence consumer spending decisions; and investors need convincing of viable opportunities.

As an individual, your personal influence in your job, business and social networks has a profound impact on your love, life and career prospects.

As a brand, if not carefully managed, a reputation that has taken years to build can be destroyed in an instant.

Great influencers, who use their skills well, increase their popularity. People like to be around them and get excited about the potential things that can happen while they are around.

They are known as doers. They don't play the victim card, moaning about things and wishing they were different. They don't blame or complain, they just get on with it.

Great influencers adapt to the situation. They modify their communication style depending on who they are talking to, but without compromising authenticity. They are able to change behaviour and attitude, not who they are!

A Moment of Reflection

So, take a moment now to ponder, maybe even sit with a blank sheet of paper and note down the answers to the following questions.

- Who has significantly influenced you over the years? List them.
- What made them influential?
- What characteristics did they display?
- Who do you influence in your life right now and why?
- Who do you want to influence in the future?
- What is the outcome you desire?

Remember, for the accompanying strategy template and other resources go to www.InfluenceTheBook.com.

INFLUENCE IN A CHANGING WORLD

The times, they are a changin'

You are quite right (well, those of you old enough), I do have Bob Dylan playing whilst I write this chapter ☺ and the words from this 1964 song title are as true today as they were then.

I believe it has never been easier to develop personal influence than it is right now. Never in the history of mankind have we enjoyed so many rich ways to communicate our message. In this chapter I want to explore some of the societal changes and how a better understanding of these changes can help you to become more influential.

And just to cement my point before I get stuck into the detail: later in this book I will touch on face-to-face communication and how a better understanding of personality types will help you identify how people like to receive information, and how knowing this helps you better communicate with them . . . now throw into the mix their social conditioning and adaptive behaviours based on their experiences of technology, exposure to media etc. All of a sudden, there is a new layer of complexity to take into account when connecting with people.

I believe becoming a student of people can massively increase your ability to influence. Understanding people's experiences and the way they view the world is essential if you want to build that connection with them.

The pace of change up until the Industrial Revolution was, to say the least, relatively slow and steady. But since then, with every technical advance, the pace of change has accelerated and continues to do so today.

Since the publication of many of the established books relating to influence, the most significant thing to happen has been the birth of the internet – the decisive technology of the information age that has connected humankind and fundamentally changed the way we interact.

> *'We are all now connected by the Internet, like neurons in a giant brain.'*
>
> **Stephen Hawking**

We live in unprecedented times when ideas can spread in an instant and generations have never been so divided.

The socialisation of technology has made the world a smaller, more competitive, place and is second nature to the digital natives, commonly referred to as 'millennials', who know no different. They were born directly into the digital age, and as a result intuitively adapt to technology changes.

With over two billion smartphone users worldwide in 2016, we have knowledge at our fingertips and the ability to connect with others in an instant. More importantly perhaps, reputations can be built or broken because anything and everything has the potential to be on the internet and on display.

As a professional speaker, my talks have to be Google proof, because every member of an audience has a computer in his or her pocket and is able to fact check everything I say, and what's more they can instantly call me out on inaccuracies by tweeting or posting online.

There is a clear divide in the attitudes, behaviours and experiences of those sharing this floating rock with us . . . And as such the things that influence us, from one person to the next, are potentially different.

For example, let's look at attitudes: if you were born after 1980 you are one of the digital natives I referred to above. Technology has probably always been a part of your life in some way, shape or form provided you live in Western society.

As a result of growing up in the last 30 years you are likely to have different attitudes to consumerism: you are less brand loyal, you rely heavily on social proof, you are getting married later, having kids later, probably have more debt etc., the list does in fact go on . . . So it stands to reason with all of these different experiences you will have different behaviours and opinions . . . What might have influenced your grandparents might not influence you.

Whilst us digital migrants (people over 35 . . . yes, me included) have adopted technology easily, it is not all we have known . . . my first exposure to computers happened in my teenage years when the Sinclair ZX81 was introduced to the marketplace. We remember a simpler time when the world did actually shut up.

If we wanted to stay on top of the news, we had to wait for it to be broadcast at specific times of the day or read our daily newspaper, which was already out of date by the time we got it.

Even then the news we did receive was undemocratic. It was the point of view of corporate media outlets with all of their biases. Compare this to today where millennials get most of their news from their peers via social media. We have access to first-hand accounts via Facebook and Twitter making it much harder for our news to be manipulated.

Another thing that has changed is our ability to focus. Our concentration spans are getting shorter and shorter with the instant gratification of consuming online in the digital age. We favour short video clips on YouTube over the time investment a TV series or movie demands.

My own kids are rarely separated from their iPhones and are constantly sharing information which has amused, inspired or moved them. In fact, the only time my son watches a TV series is when he can consume multiple episodes at once via Netflix, because waiting a week for the next episode is sooooo last century.

We went from communication that required thought and formatting, letters and emails . . . to the texting and 140 character bastardisation of language which has reduced our ability to express ourselves to an emoji. To quote Donald Trump: #Sad.

A recent survey of Canadian media consumption, conducted by technology giant Microsoft, concluded that the average attention span had fallen to just 8 seconds, down from 12 seconds in the year 2000. This is one second less than a goldfish.

Attention span, according to Wikipedia, can be defined as *'the amount of concentrated time one can spend on a task without becoming distracted.'* But we live in distracting times! It's no wonder we find it harder to concentrate.

> *'A good teacher, like a good entertainer first must hold his audience's attention, then he can teach his lesson.'*
>
> **John Henrik Clarke**

I believe human attention will be one of the scarcest commodities of the very near future, but essential for influence. If we are to hold attention long enough to share our message, we have to change the way we communicate.

So why do I share all of this? Mainly because I really want to hammer home the point that we need to continuously adapt the way we communicate if we want to influence – because it isn't one size fits all, and what works today may not work tomorrow.

If the audience you are trying to influence is spread across multi demographics, yet you are using one tone of voice, or one platform to communicate, the chances are you are not speaking to everyone.

A Moment of Reflection

So reflecting on this change, and your answers from the previous section where you identified who you influence right now and who you would like to influence in the future, consider the following.

- What demographic do they belong to (age, sex, ideology, class, location etc.)?
- What influences them right now (people, media, brands, publications etc.)?
- What is important to them?
- Where do they congregate both online and offline?
- Where do they consume?

Remember, for the accompanying strategy template and other resources go to www.InfluenceTheBook.com.

SETTING OBJECTIVES FOR INFLUENCE

Before I share with you what I consider the key principles of influence, I wanted to talk a little about objectives and strategy.

Now this isn't a book about goal setting, so I am not going to go into too much detail about how to effectively set goals – although for those interested, at the end of this chapter, I will give you my summary take on setting SMART goals which you can use if you like.

Clearly you bought this book for a reason, and you may already have a desired outcome, though maybe not a detailed plan.

Whatever your objectives, there will be things you can do to influence your success. There will also be people you can influence to help you achieve them.

Ask yourself

- What are my influence goals?
- Who needs to be influenced to achieve this goal (people or brands)?
- How do they need to be influenced, i.e. desired behaviour?
- What is my desired outcome?
- What channels of influence are open to me to reach them?
- What publications (online and offline) would provide useful profiles?
- What speaking opportunities help me target this audience?
- Which other influencers might be able to help me?
- What potential partnerships could be formed in the pursuit of this goal?

- What websites would it be useful to have a presence on to reach this audience?

By all means take some time now to think through these questions, and better still write down your answers. As you proceed through the book new ideas will present themselves, so you can refine your thinking and develop your strategy.

Here is a quick guide to setting SMART goals for those unfamiliar with what they are. There are several variations for the acronym which are listed here, I will be using the words in bold.

S	**Specific**, stretching, significant
M	**Measurable**, motivational, meaningful
A	attainable, **Achievable**, acceptable, action-oriented, agreed upon, accountable
R	realistic, **Relevant**, reasonable, results-oriented, rewarding
T	time-based, **Time-bound**, timely, tangible, trackable

Specific

When setting goals, you need to be as specific as you can to improve your chances of success. Where possible use the six Ws;

Who	Who is involved?
What	What do you want to accomplish?
Where	Where will this take place?
When	When will this happen (establish your time frame)?
Which	How will you do this (which requirements/constraints stand between you and your goal)?
Why	Why are you doing this (what is your purpose for this goal)?

For example, a general goal would be to 'write more'. A specific goal would be to 'Write one 1000-word blog every week for the next year to increase my content, improve my writing skills and drive traffic to my website.'

Measurable

By setting measurable goals you will stay focused and know how to track your progress. Establish your criteria using questions like how much . . .? How many . . .? How will I know when the task is complete?

Agreed upon

Make sure all stakeholders agree on what the outcome should be and the timescales for completion. This makes you more accountable and increases your chances of success.

Realistic

If your goals are unachievable you will just give up. If they are too easy you will lack motivation. Setting goals that stretch you – but are with in the realms of possibility with available resources, knowledge and time – are the best to keep you motivated.

Time-based

A goal should be grounded with in a time frame which will provide you with a sense of urgency. What's your deadline? What are your milestones?

THE PRINCIPLES OF INFLUENCE

I set out to write this book because I think that previous writings in this genre tend to focus on persuasion techniques and don't cover other areas which are key to becoming influential. Keep in mind they were written before the digital age, which redefined influence and changed the way we source information.

So, in this next section of my book, I want to share some of the key principles I have used successfully throughout my career; sometimes knowingly, and sometimes accidentally (and only indentified upon reflection).

In the following section we will explore further how we apply these principles in everyday situations and, in order to help you make the most of this book, at the end of each section I will summarise the key learning and ask you a few questions to help contextualise the lessons for you.

I have broken these principles down into five categories using the acronym P.I.C.K.Y., which as a word means to be meticulous, to demand to have things just right, to care about the details. When it comes to your influence strategy, these seem appropriate traits.

This is what P.I.C.K.Y. stands for.

*P*eople	The people you need to influence.
*I*mage	The image you portray both online and offline.
*C*ommunication	Effective communication to influence.
*K*nowledge	What you know and how best to share it.
*Y*ou	The characteristics of great influencers.

2

P IS FOR PEOPLE

Who do you know and, more importantly, who knows you?

Ultimately, every part of this book relates to people. It is people who influence us through their messages delivered across many different media. But in this section of the book I want to talk about people in the context of relationships.

YOUR NETWORK

Your network is the most important factor in determining your future success, the age-old adage of '*It isn't what you know, but who you know*' I believe is largely true. The better your network is, the better the opportunities available to you.

When talking about your influence, I would add '*It isn't what you know, or who you know . . . It is who knows you.*' And it is influence that opens doors.

Many years ago, I ran an event management business and our target market was large corporate firms. In the town where we were based there was a lot of industry with many international firms running their HQs from there.

Having spent a lot of time trying to get into these companies without any luck we knew we needed to take a different approach.

My business partner at the time had ties to the local football club which had recently been promoted to the Premiership (the UK's highest professional league) and had been approached by the club's goalkeeper, Fraser Digby, who was coming to the end of his playing career and was looking to pursue a business career.

Needless to say, we snapped him up; after all he was a local legend and extremely popular around the town.

Suddenly, every company we had previously approached but had rejected us, started to invite us in. Now Fraser was a gentle giant, very charming and very comfortable socially. But he knew nothing about our business or the industry in general, so our strategy was to go in and let Fraser charm the pants off them before I would take over to talk business. It worked a treat.

You see, Fraser's influence opened the door. He didn't necessarily know them, but they knew him. That was all we needed.

A good network can open doors for you, but the vast majority of people I see networking are doing it wrong. The number of events I've attended or run where I've witnessed people simply trying to collect data, i.e. exchange a business card, without any desire to put effort into the relationship.

Given the choice I would go for deep and narrow over broad and shallow every time. It is the depth of a relationship that creates trust and it is only with trust that the best opportunities arise.

Most people, when they think about networking, make the mistake of seeing it only as a marketing strategy for finding new customers. I have always found this limiting. For me, my network is a source of guidance, it is critical feedback on our ideas or the issues we face. Our most powerful connections will probably never do business with us, but with the right time invested in the relationship, they will help us with introductions and guidance.

Thirty years ago, networking wasn't even a chapter in a marketing book, let alone the multi-billion dollar industry it is today if we include online. Now, we not only understand the importance of a good network, but it has never been easier to connect with people worldwide due to the new relationship economy we live in, and the social technology which supports it.

For the ambitious employee, or budding entrepreneur, cultivating strong relationships with the right people could be the single most important strategy for your career or business progress.

Throughout this book there are lessons you can apply when in a networking situation – but remember, building your network isn't just about networking events or using LinkedIn. Keep your eyes and ears open all the time.

Serendipity has been kind to me over the years, providing valuable connections in random situations – including someone who simply overheard me speaking on a train and subsequently became an investor. What has made it easy for me to spot great contacts and build relationships quickly boils down to two things.

1. I want to be of service to my network, so I both listen and connect where appropriate. This creates reciprocity (more on this later).

2. I remind myself constantly of my wants and needs so they are always front of mind.

When your needs are front of mind, it is so much easier to spot the opportunities that relate to them. For example, have you ever bought a new car and on your way home spotted the same model everywhere? They were always there; it is just that your awareness is heightened. So, in order to be a better opportunist, write down your objectives and revisit them often.

A Moment of Reflection

- Where do you network right now?
- What other local opportunities exist?
- What industry opportunities exist?
- Who are the people running influential networks relevant to you? Could you connect with them right now?

Remember, for the accompanying strategy template and other resources go to www.InfluenceTheBook.com.

THE LAW OF RECIPROCITY

Proactive connecting – becoming the hub

Have you ever experienced the feeling of wanting to do something for someone simply because they have at some point done something for you? Even if they haven't asked?

Social psychologists call this phenomenon 'The Law of Reciprocity', and it is essentially our deep-rooted desire to help those who help us. Often you may reciprocate with a gesture far more generous than their original act of kindness.

Conversely, in response to hostile actions, people are often much nastier and, in some cases, even brutal. This can, if unchecked, cause a spiral of negativity which is probably the reason why conflicts escalate due to the constant need for retribution from each side.

If the above is true (which it is), then it is surely advantageous to understand this powerful social law. This is a law which can be abused by someone with bad intentions. However, as I will discuss later, the people who abuse it rarely endure when it comes to influence – and are found out eventually.

Let us first discuss the right and wrong way to use this law.

First, the right way. When trying to establish a new relationship, we focus our energies on building rapport and ultimately trust. So, to demonstrate, as one of life's good guys there are a number of things you can do like listen, be helpful, smile, be honest, generous and transparent.

This is a common technique used by online marketers who share freely something which has genuine value without asking for anything in return (except maybe your email address ;-))

By giving away these materials they are demonstrating expertise, showing they understand the pain and are willing to help, and lastly they are showing that they are not only after your money.

By doing this they have invoked the law of reciprocity. You now perceive them to be trustworthy and generous and will be more inclined to spend with them when they have something to offer.

When people use the law the wrong way it feels like manipulation: a coercive exploitative tactic which can usually be spotted a mile away but, should you fall for it, leaves a bad aftertaste.

I remember one time I was walking in London, on the phone, when it started to rain. So, I took shelter in a department store whilst I finished my call. As I hung up the phone my hand was taken by a beautiful woman and I was led to the cosmetics counter and invited to take a seat. I had some time to kill before my next meeting and was curious as to what would happen next, so I went along with it.

She showed me my eyes in a mirror and, as I am the wrong side of 40, there are one or two lines starting to appear. The next thing I know she is rubbing – or rather massaging – a cream into my eyes to reduce the wrinkles. In that moment, I forgot all my troubles, relaxed and enjoyed the attention.

When she finished, she showed me my eyes again and there was a visible difference which, for all I know, could have been down to the massage. She then asked if I would like to buy the cream. Something inside me felt obligated to say yes, I didn't even ask the price. A moment later, and £56 lighter, I was walking away with the smallest jar of cream imaginable, which to this day sits unopened on a shelf in my bathroom.

I might have been upset by this experience, mad at myself for not saying no and seeing through this deliberate ploy to make me buy. But I'm not. Every time I see the jar it reminds me to avoid this well used sales tactic in future.

In the main, when someone uses the law of reciprocity in this way it is obvious; and in the long term it is not good for your brand. It certainly won't generate you any good will or repeat business. But in today's digital age a pressured prospect can make a lot of noise.

So as long as you apply this law with integrity and for the right reasons, it can be a powerful technique for developing relationships.

Oh and by the way, by delivering a service that goes above and beyond the call of duty you can also achieve similar results – and the reciprocation is customer loyalty and referrals!

BECOMING A CONNECTOR

Let's look at this in the context of your network. In Malcolm Gladwell's awesome book *Tipping Point* he discusses certain people in the world he calls 'connectors'. These are people who instinctively bring people together without any direct or obvious benefit to themselves.

Being a connector can generate an enormous amount of good will and is a relatively easy thing to master. The more you understand your network, its wants and needs, the better positioned you are to help it. Every time you connect two people your credibility increases in both of their eyes. Just be careful to make the right connections as this can backfire.

Several years ago, my business partner and I were introduced to someone by a trusted contact. We met and liked them and, on the surface, there appeared to be a significant opportunity on the table. But something wasn't right.

We couldn't shake this feeling, so before we committed any cash we decided to have this person looked into. This was the first time in my career I had ever hired a private investigator and, on this occasion, it was money well spent: it was a scam!

Why do I share this? Well, remember, this was an introduction from a trusted friend and there were only two conclusions we could come to.

1. They were complicit in the scam, in which case our relationship was damaged forever, or

2. They were well-intentioned but oblivious to the scam.

I am pleased to say we eventually discovered it was the latter and, on this occasion, we didn't fall for it. But what if we had? As it happens another contact of ours *had* fallen for it and was significantly out of pocket. Their response was not so forgiving, and as a result reputations were damaged.

Becoming a connector is a powerful way to build reciprocity, but don't make the mistake of expecting something in return. You will spot those that just wish to use you by simply taking advantage of your good will. True colours always shine through. Mostly people will want to help you with your needs in return.

Whenever someone new to networking asks for my advice, I always encourage them to be the hub. Be the go-to person when others want introductions. Being the hub puts you at the centre of other people's networks and keeps you front of mind.

A simple way to apply this or get started is to volunteer to help at a networking event; or better still organise one yourself. As one of the organisers, people will come to you for introductions and you become more authoritative in the eyes of the visitors simply by being the one in charge.

Know your network

To become an awesome connector, know your network. By this I mean remember every introduction you receive and make sure you show your gratitude.

To illustrate why this is important I want to share a story. When I started my first network/business community, I made a point of getting to know all of the national players in the networking space in the UK and beyond.

I struck a friendship with many network heads, and in particular a chap by the name of Andy Lopata (who now consults for big brands on networking and is an accomplished speaker on the subject). Andy took the time to introduce me to his regional team and, in turn, I took the time to travel and meet them.

One evening whilst sat at home I received a call from Andy's regional leader from Birmingham. He was at an event with someone and wanted to introduce me. This person was Bill Morrow, Founder of AngelsDen.com, now an international brand and crowdfunding platform.

Bill and I spoke on the phone and arranged to meet in London the following week, where we really hit it off. Over the coming weeks he introduced me to some exceptional people, including the programme director from the Telegraph Business Club who we went on to form a media partnership with. Through them we went on to win a significant amount of sponsorship from a variety of household brands, the biggest of which was £100k with Alliance & Leicester (now Santander).

So why tell you all of this? Well, in that anecdote alone there is a trail of six different introductions, which all started with Andy Lopata. Had he not made the first intro, none of the events that followed would have ever happened. He was instrumental in our early success without even knowing it. Until of course I told him and made sure he understood how grateful we were.

This teaches us never to underestimate the potential of an introduction and to ensure we always recognise when someone takes the time to connect us, and also to reciprocate wherever possible.

A Moment of Reflection

- Take some time to explore your network on LinkedIn. Examine what groups people are part of, what events they attend and who they know in turn.
- Think about people you can connect within your network that could add value to each other. Take some time to make those introductions.
- Schedule some time to leave properly considered testimonials for your key contacts. Not only will they be grateful, they may reciprocate and it will start a dialogue.
- Who are the key connectors in your network? Why not organise a coffee or attend an event you know they will be at?
- What events would it be useful for you to get involved in? Any one of them could be a step towards being the hub.

Remember, for the accompanying strategy template and other resources go to www.InfluenceTheBook.com.

CREDIBILITY BY ASSOCIATION

Being known by the company you keep

> *'You are the average of the five people you spend the most time with.'*
>
> **Jim Rohn**

Credibility by association is the simple premise that we are known by the company we keep. If we are seen rubbing shoulders with highly respected leaders, there is a perception that we too are important. This also works on a brand level.

One of my favourite examples of someone really understanding credibility by association is from a well-known Scottish speaker by the name of Jack Black (no, not the chubby comedic Hollywood actor. ;-)

Jack was a social worker in the 1980s but had a huge interest in personal development. Whilst consuming others' material he was also developing his own and he reached a point where he was ready to start sharing it.

With absolute faith in the quality of his material, Jack borrowed over £10,000 to hire Sir John Harvey Jones MBE to come and deliver a speech in front of a Glaswegian audience. Due to his successful TV show with the BBC, called *Troubleshooter*, Sir John was a popular, no-nonsense business figure and a huge draw attracting over 2000 business leaders to the event.

For Jack this was a very clever move, not only had he recouped his investment through ticket sales, he also immediately built credibility by association simply by being the other person on stage. Of course he needed to deliver great content himself, it's not enough to just be seen with the right people, you need substance too. Jack went on to build a multi-million-pound business consulting with corporates across the world as well as working with national sports teams on their mindset.

It was many years later when I discovered Jack Black. My wife's company had put her through his Mindstore programme and she had brought some of the materials home with her on a cassette (remember those?), which she thought I would like due to my interest in personal development.

I listened to the tape, and immediately became interested both in the content and in connecting with Jack. Without hesitation, I reached out and requested a meeting. To my surprise I was invited to fly to Glasgow to meet him at the airport.

Now I flew from Bristol, where there was only an early morning flight there and an early evening flight back. Our meeting was to take place at the hotel right next to the terminal, so I was going to have a lot of time to kill.

I remember the meeting very clearly because it taught me two very important lessons which I have never forgotten. The first lesson relates to being prepared when you meet busy influential people for the first time.

You see, I arrived knowing I wanted to work with Jack, but with no real plan, proposal or idea of what that might look like. Within the first five minutes of the meeting, once the pleasantries were out of the way, he asked me what I was looking to achieve from the meeting. While giving him my answer my brain was screaming 'you IDIOT Warren!' I had done the hard work and got the meeting . . . but had turned up woefully underprepared to actually turn it into something.

My reply was 'I have come with an open mind to see if there is something we could do.' Idiot. Now, Jack was gracious, but I could see the micro expression of disappointment and knew I had blown it. Bless him, he gave me an hour and coached me on the best way to approach him in future (which I did) and I learned an important lesson: before you go into any meeting in future, know what your desired outcome is.

This is especially true of important people; they are time-poor and in demand. Make sure you don't create a first impression of wasting their time!

The next thing that happened really cemented the principle of credibility by association. As Jack left the hotel, I was approached by another gentleman. He said to me, 'Excuse me, I couldn't help but notice you were just talking with Jack Black. Can I buy you a coffee?'

We of course had a coffee, after all I had hours to kill. Followed by lunch. It turns out we were on the same flight where we sat together, all this time building a deeper connection. It won't surprise you to hear we later did business, but none of that would have happened had I not been sat with someone he greatly admired.

Credibility by association works on so many levels, and later in this book we will explore different scenarios.

This is a principle which is not just restricted to people, it works with brands too.

In 2006, I started an online business community which also brought people together in the real world for networking . . . I briefly touched on it in the last chapter. We understood at the time that if we could attract a couple of bigger brands to sponsor us we would increase our credibility and, of course, improve cash flow.

I approached several brands and the first to seriously bite was the telecoms giant O2. Their interest was to have more conversations with small business owners and they recognised our potential to facilitate this through our events and online forums.

Six months later, we were still struggling to get the deal over the line, which was frustrating, mainly because I didn't know why it was taking so long. Then something happened which changed things in an instant. Alongside this deal, we had been working on a media partnership with the UK national newspaper the *Daily Telegraph* (yes, as a result of the Andy Lopata introduction), specifi-cally with their business club.

Within two weeks the O2 deal was signed, and we later learned that they were just nervous because we were unknown. They knew they were going to be the first brand to work with us, and we simply had not built up enough credibility for the decision makers within O2 to be comfortable. With the support of a national news-paper, those fears went away.

You see, most people don't realise or consider that behind every sponsorship deal you will ever see, is a human being within a company who has made a decision for which they can be held accountable.

Well, as soon as the first big brand came on board, we witnessed a domino effect with other brands coming to the table with much shorter negotiation times.

There is a BUT!!!

Actually, in this case there are two buts.

But number one: credibility by association is only good for starting a relationship. You still have to develop your own credibility in order to sustain it in the long run. What does this mean?

Well, it means you still need to have the right values, the right knowledge, the right ambition and achieve the right results by taking action.

Are you the type of person who adapts and persists? Who when faced with adversity overcomes it? Or do you quit and blame everything but yourself? Long-term credibility and influence come from you; your actions not someone else's. So be worthy!

But number two: credibility by association also has a flipside, guilty by association.

You are walking down a street and you come across a man sat with a sign saying 'Homeless, Broke and Hungry'. You reach into your pocket to find some money to help this person in need, when suddenly you hear his phone ring. You stop and watch as he takes a call and has a conversation. When his call finishes, he packs up his sign, walks around the corner and gets into his new car and drives off.

How does this make you feel? Obviously, this man is running a scam.

Now, later that day, you stumble across another man with a similar sign. Can you honestly say the thought wouldn't cross your mind that this is possibly another scam? It may be that this is a genuine case of someone in need, but your previous experience has tarnished the second man's credibility.

Credibility by association really does work both ways. The Jim Rohn quote 'You are the average of the five people you spend most time with' also means 'be careful of your relationships'. A good example of this is Hillary Clinton who, with her husband, has spent 40 years in the public limelight. Over this time, they have built more than a dozen relationships with friends, co-workers and business associates who have turned out to be criminals, thieves, investment conmen – even an underage sex offender – and agents of foreign influence. Many of these have been to prison.

At the time of writing, Hillary is one of the most unpopular presidential candidates of all time with a nickname of 'Crooked Hillary' and lucky to be up against someone who is even more unpopular and equally guilty by association.

Of course, you will have heard of many sports stars losing lucrative sponsorship/endorsement deals because of their bad behaviour. From Mike Tyson (Pepsi) to Tiger Woods (Gillette, Accenture, AT&T, Gatorade and Tag Heuer), Wayne Rooney (Coca-Cola) and more recently US swimmer Ryan Lochte who lost his four commercial sponsors (Speedo, Ralph Lauren, Airweave and Gentle Hair Removal) after being caught in a lie following an incident at the Rio de Janeiro Olympic Games.

So, the lesson is: think carefully about the company you keep, but ultimately be worthy of your own credibility!

A Moment of Reflection

- Who are the established names within your organisation, industry, networks and the media that, would serve you well to build a relationship with?
- Who do you already know well enough to approach for mentoring?
- What relevant and established brands have great credibility in your niche, that you might be able to partner/collaborate with?
- What customers do you already have that a well worded testimonial or case study from would increase your credibility?

Remember, for the accompanying strategy template and other resources go to www.InfluenceTheBook.com.

IDENTIFYING AND APPROACHING INFLUENCERS

So, we now understand that we can bask in the reflective glow of influential people whilst working on our own credibility. But how do we attract influencers in the first place? Here are a few ideas for you.

The term 'influencer marketing' is a form of marketing widely used by retailers, manufacturers and brands where the focus is on specific key individuals as opposed to the market as a whole. These key individuals can exert powerful influence over potential buyers. This is not what I am talking about here, although it is a fascinating subject. What I'm saying is that as individuals, looking to grow our personal influence, we can learn a few lessons and, more importantly, apply them.

A great influencer for you is generally one who is relevant to your objectives. For example, if you are the ambitious employee, it could be senior people within your organisation or respected people within your industry.

If you are a local business, it could be well-connected business leaders in the area, or the business editor in your local newspaper, or the head of your local chamber of commerce (depending on what you sell).

If you are a consultant, it could be someone respected in your industry association . . . you get the point.

If you are not sure who your target influencers are then there are numerous online resources you can use, as well as the basic search tools on most social sites. But really, if you are not sure who they are, then you might not yet be ready to connect with them. Do your research.

I have listed some additional resources for identifying influencers on my website which should prove useful.

The type of approach you might want to make will be dictated by the person you are approaching and what you would like to achieve with the relationship. But one thing I urge you to do is to be clear in advance on what your objective is and how it is also in their interests to connect with you.

So, with all of that said, I would like to share with you seven key rules when making an approach to influential people.

Before I start, by the way, the end goal or perfect outcome you are looking for is to develop a meaningful relationship, not just a photo opportunity. Your barometer for success is whether you are remembered and respected.

Rule One: Don't ask for anything

This is rule one for a reason. It is important!

Influential people by their very nature are busy and in demand. They are inundated with requests for their time and attention and the last thing you want to be doing in your first interaction is asking for something.

I have several friends who are considered famous or wealthy and the one common thing they share is how tired they are of people trying to get money from them or leverage their fame. I know at least one celebrity who has actually become quite lonely as a result of this and is cynical of nearly everyone's intentions.

A much better reason to want to connect with influential people is to learn from them. The very fact that they are influential means they are probably highly accomplished and extremely knowledgeable. Their conversation will be rich and their lessons will hopefully inspire you.

Rule Two: Add value to them

I have always found that if you approach someone with a genuine desire to help them, their guard will drop and the potential for the relationship will increase. But you mustn't expect something in return.

I once got the opportunity to meet Guy Kawasaki with my friend, the talented author Sarah Arrow. We spent a decent amount of time interviewing him with a view to reviewing and blogging about his latest book *Enchantment*.

Our value add was to raise awareness of his book to our audiences; and in return we got to listen to the insights and observations of a great thought leader.

Rule Three: Communicate on their level

No one likes a sycophant! As a public speaker, I regularly leave the stage to be greeted by members of the audience who want to talk with me and will queue to do so. It is very flattering and I am privileged to be able to share my ideas with them. But they typically fall into four categories:

Star Struck   Nice people who are in awe of you, seem to genuinely appreciate you (which is great) but lack the confidence to speak as your equal.

Sycophantic   A person who praises people to gain their approval. Usually just a self-serving flatterer!

Insecure and Rude   This person goes out of their way to tell you how good they are and acts way too cool due to their own insecurities.

Self-Secure   Typically respectful, but also aware of the value they bring and not afraid to share their own experiences. They communicate very much as your equal.

It will not surprise you to know that the self-secure are the ones influencers see as on the same level as themselves and the only ones with the potential to become friends.

Rule Four: Have social proof

We live in an age of due diligence and you can bet your bottom dollar you are being checked out on a regular basis. I am going to cover social proof in more detail later in the book, but in the context of reaching out to influencers . . . *evidence of integrity* is important. A well populated LinkedIn profile with plenty of endorsements and testimonials is useful – and you can help yourself by making it easy to find by being obvious on your website or in your email signature. After all, their professional reputations are on the line.

Rule Five: Introductions increase odds

It is very rare that a direct approach will work when reaching out to influential people. They often have gatekeepers who fiercely protect them from distractions. It is far better to be introduced by someone already trusted.

It can be much easier to build bridging relationships initially and, although it might take longer, you will have a better chance of success.

Two things you can do to make this process easier: first, make quality introductions yourself; if you know two influencers who are not yet connected but might benefit from knowing each other, introduce them. This way you are adding value as per rule two.

Second, make introducing you easy. If asking for an introduction, write the paragraph for the introducer. This helps to contextualise the reason for it and is more likely to be well received and followed up on.

Rule Six: The magic of mentors

To be clear, I am not for one instant saying you should approach cold, as a stranger, a person of influence and ask them to be your mentor. That wouldn't work.

However, if you are lucky enough to develop a relationship over time (i.e. several conversations), which evolves into a mentor/mentee relationship then this could be a great source of other influential introductions.

This starts with humility . . . no one wants to mentor a know-it-all. And be very aware: when a mentor introduces you to someone, you represent their reputation, so make them look good!

Rule Seven: Don't bullshit

Admit when you don't know. Really bullshit doesn't baffle brains and accomplished people have a better bullshit radar than most.

As I have said, we live in an age where everything you say has to be Google proof and can be tested with our pocket oracles aka smartphones.

So, don't try to big up yourself or be too clever. People see through it.

Getting noticed by influential people

Lastly, an easy way to develop relationships with influencers is to become one yourself and get noticed. Here are a few ideas to get noticed.

- Have something to say and say it often.
- Write a blog, get published and demonstrate expertise (see Knowledge section).
- Be shareable (and share yourself).
- Niche your knowledge – it is ok to operate in multiple niches, but to build real influence is to go deep and narrow.
- Consider public speaking, it's a fast track to authority and you are more likely to get noticed at industry events (see Knowledge section).

With all of the above, you get to build relationships with fellow speakers, bloggers and publishers. Chances are they have a decent black book of their own.

THE POWER OF PARTNERSHIPS

In our increasingly interconnected society, your competition could be in the next street or on the other side of the world. Partnerships are an effective way to maintain a competitive advantage; by combining skills and expertise, we can ensure we stay relevant to the needs of our customers.

Credibility by association is a major benefit when creating partnerships or joint ventures. Think about it, if you are launching a new business or even just expanding into a new industry/niche etc., what better way to do it than to partner with someone already established in that industry?

Partnering isn't only an advantage for larger companies. The term 'joint venture' (JV) was traditionally used for large companies creating new legal entities to take new products or services to market. But today the term is used more casually by entrepreneurs in relation to smaller collaborative projects.

Whilst a partnership can be defined in several ways, for me it is simply two or more entities, collaborating in a structured way to achieve an agreed outcome.

A number of factors may vary within my definition, namely the entities (individual or organisation etc.), the structure of the relationship (contracted, new legal entity etc.) and of course the desired outcomes, which may not be the same for all parties.

There are many benefits to partnerships, here are but a few:

- increasing your reach by combining your networks,
- mutual endorsement – cross referrals,
- combining your capabilities,
- reduced overheads,
- media attention,
- increased profile,
- credibility by association and
- more opportunities.

So, having been sold on the benefits, how should you go about selecting the right partners?

This is actually really important to get right if you want to achieve something meaningful and avoid disputes. Here are a few areas to think about when seeking the right partners and, more importantly, making partnerships work.

Values   Take time to identify people or organisations whose values are aligned with your own. Whether those are values underpinned by morality (honesty, integrity etc.) or relating to people (customer service, respect, personal development etc.) or even the practical things relating to implementation (innovation, accountability, detail oriented). A word of warning: getting this wrong could impact your reputation.

Relevancy   Seeking partners with complementary skills or assets is wholly sensible. In relation to influence, it may be that you simply extend each other's reach to your respective audiences.

Mutual Benefit   If one partner gains significantly more from a relationship it can be a cause of conflict. Hopefully this will be something you have already thought about and compensated for. If you really want a long-term partnership, seek win–win arrangements.

Establish the Ground Rules   Establishing the way you are going to work together, and managing each other's expectations up front, is essential. Avoid assumptions and really spell out how you would like the partnership to work.

Communication is Key   Research suggests that the number one reason for breakdown in partnerships is poor communications. Seek clarity at all times and establish regular times to discuss progress.

A Moment of Reflection

- Who are your competitors? List them.
- Who operates in your industry or services your clients, but may be in a different field? Preferably complementary.
- Think about what a partnership could look like with these brands. Where would the value exchange be? What could each party bring to the table?
- What would each party look to gain from the relationship?
- Who has great penetration/reach into your market even if they are simply a media outlet?

Remember, for the accompanying strategy template and other resources go to www.InfluenceTheBook.com.

CREATING ADVOCACY

The most talked about influencers are those that create advocacy, enabling their network, customers and raving fans to refer them.

This doesn't just work for people running their own business. If you are an ambitious employee looking to rise through the ranks within your company, you can accelerate the process by simply building stronger relationships with the colleagues that already have influence or are recognised as having potential.

I know a chap who is now on the board of an international company, a household brand, and has worked his way up since joining as a graduate many years ago. He was given this advice back then and did two things straight away: first he asked for mentorship from established people in the company. No one refused him, in fact in my experience it is very flattering to be asked to mentor. Successful leaders want to nurture talent. By having influential people within the organisation as a mentor he got to develop a stronger, deeper relationship with them and naturally, when more senior roles became available, his name was on all of their lips.

Advocacy earned will always be far more valuable than advocacy bought

We all understand that the best reason to advocate a brand is that we love it. For example, have you ever discussed buying a Windows laptop in proximity to a Mac user?

Apple fans will literally queue in all weathers, through the night if necessary, for the latest gadget, and pay a premium for it too. That is love you just can't buy.

Focus on your relationships

According to research conducted by Deloitte, customers that are referred by other customers have a 37% higher retention rate, and are more likely to convert in the first place.

Staying engaged and staying front of mind is the best way to focus on your relationships. Speak to your network regularly and keep them informed of your developments. Educate them on how you add value to your customers so it is your name that springs to mind when they encounter someone with the same needs.

Go above and beyond

'Referrals are very powerful. When I refer you, I give a little bit of my reputation away. If you do a good job, my friend that hired you is pleased. But if you do a bad job, that reflects badly on me. People forget that.'

Ivan Misner

The above quote by Ivan Misner sums up what I believe is a really important point when growing advocacy. When you get referred by someone, it is your obligation to go above and beyond to make them look like a super hero.

Firstly, your referrer has put their neck on the line and the best way to thank them is to make them look great for making the referral in the first place by exceeding expectations.

But by going above and beyond for your customers you will create yet more advocates because you are worth talking about. Consider surprising them with unexpected benefits and adding more value.

A friend of mine, David Gilroy, runs a company called Conscious Solutions from Bristol, UK. Now Conscious have a strong position in their marketplace providing exceptional websites for the legal profession.

On a regular basis I hear from David about the latest value-add initiative they've created for their customers. As a brand they really live and breathe their values, it determines their every decision and they really have the wow factor. As a result, they consistently grow and their customers are fans.

What do you do that makes you worth talking about?

Also, remember to say thank you to your advocates. I mean properly. Take them to lunch or include them in a hospitality event. Even just a personal message for supporting you. This recognition can go a long way to cementing their support and can drive future referrals.

Enable your advocates

Make it easy for your advocates to help you by ensuring you have sharing options on your website and social content. Echo their praises by sharing within your social streams, developing their advocacy even further. Give them a shout out #LoveYourFans.

Measure and reward

To truly understand the effectiveness of your advocacy strategy, make sure you have simple tools in place to monitor where your new leads are coming from.

Of course, this is easier to do for online advocates with analytics, but ask the following questions.

- Who shares your content or produces content about you?
- Who are your biggest influencers?
- What are they saying to their followers?
- Where are they saying it?
- What content is shared the most?
- How is that responded to by their audience?
- Why are they sharing your content?

Remember, creating a successful advocacy programme is a medium- to long-term strategy. The most important thing to remember is to make time for developing the relationships and keeping them engaged.

Show appreciation regularly and don't take your advocates for granted.

A Moment of Reflection

- What could you do right now to add more value to your customers?
- What would it take to get more engaged with your customers?
- Do you make it easy for others to refer you?
- Do you incentivise and reward people for referrals?
- When you receive referrals, how do you go above and beyond?
- When you receive referrals, how do you say thank you?

Remember, for the accompanying strategy template and other resources go to www.InfluenceTheBook.com.

BECOME A STUDENT OF PEOPLE – START WITH YOU

Psychology and behavioural sciences are becoming increasingly valued as a source of knowledge for personal development, business growth and managing relationships.

I have always been keen to develop my self-awareness and really appreciate it as a quality in other people. There are several free tests online which I have listed on my blog, so no excuses.

By starting with yourself you are far better positioned to recognise the characteristics of the people you seek to motivate and influence.

When it comes to influence, understanding your own personality is useful for developing leadership, empathy and motivation. Better still, this helps you improve your own ability to relate to others.

You may be familiar with the DISC model which is the foundation for various tests in the marketplace. One I particularly like is Ensize which explores adaptive behaviours too, i.e. the way our behaviour varies based on our environmental influences.

My good friend Michelle Mills Porter, who heads up Ensize in the UK, believes the personality theories that underpin personality tests are surprisingly easy to understand at a basic level. She explains that you can quickly assess a person simply by deciding whether they are introvert or extrovert, and then deciding whether they are task oriented or people oriented.

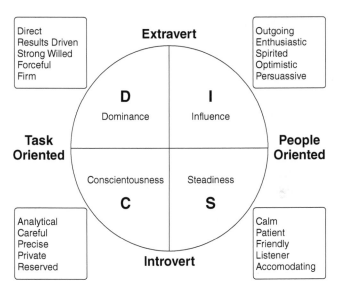

Figure 2.1

With this knowledge, you can make an educated guess around how they like to receive information, which is a useful advantage when meeting someone for the first time, especially someone you would like to influence.

Figure 2.1, alongside the list below, show details of the DISC model.

Extroverted and people oriented Someone who is extrovert and people oriented is optimistic and sociable. Keeping the conversation fun and positive is a great way to build rapport with them.

Extroverted and task oriented Someone who is extrovert and task oriented is direct and decisive. They prefer to get to the point and like immediate results.

Introverted and people oriented Someone who is introvert and people oriented is a supportive team player. With them, demonstrate you have the team's best interests at heart, speak calmly and avoid confrontation.

Introverted and task oriented Someone who is introvert and task oriented is cautious and focused on accuracy. With them, avoid ambiguity and stick to the facts.

Understanding personality types is helpful for appreciating that, while people are different, we all have values, strengths and qualities.

Often, when it comes to communication, there are conflicts, we don't always get along or have compatible communication styles. But it is important to understand that people very rarely set out to cause upset, they just behave differently because they *are* different.

Whoever you are and whatever you want to achieve, I recommend taking at least one psychometric test to get a better understanding of your behaviours and communication preferences. Then try adapting your communication style to mirror those you wish to develop relationships with.

A Moment of Reflection

- Take some time to try a couple of free online tests right now (listed on my blog).
- Reflect on your strengths and weaknesses, especially when it comes to communication.
- Think about some of your key contacts, using the simple model above. What category would you put them in?
- Reflect on how you have communicated with them in the past. What would you now do differently?
- Think about some of the people you have struggled to get along with in the past? Where do they potentially fit?
- How would you communicate differently to improve your relationship?

Remember, for the accompanying strategy template and other resources go to www.InfluenceTheBook.com.

3

I IS FOR IMAGE

When growing your influence, it is essential to understand your image . . . not to be confused by your brand.

In my humble opinion, after years of supporting small business owners, I have come to the conclusion that the vast majority of them don't understand the importance of their brand or image and it is very unlikely they understand the difference between the two.

Establishing yourself in the marketplace, differentiating from your competitors and staying front of mind are all dependent on your brand and your image.

A brand is a company's identity in the market, building awareness with customers and helping them to be distinguishable from the competition.

I have heard it said that the best way to identify a brand is to pretend you can't read. As an example, you walk into a food court at a shopping mall and are presented with two choices for something to eat. One of them has golden arches and the other one has a white-haired colonel with a red apron.

I am pretty sure you have now identified them as McDonald's and KFC. What else do you know about them? What food do they serve? What price can you expect to pay? What is it like inside? Both have successfully established their brands so you as the consumer know exactly what to expect.

A company image is more personal and relates more to how consumers feel about your business and, maybe more specifically, you.

For example, let's come back to KFC: you may feel it is a tasty, affordable, family friendly place to eat, or you may object to their farming methods and be concerned about the welfare of the millions of chickens they use. Whilst the brand is easily recognisable, how you feel about it is totally subjective.

So, in this section of the book I want to focus on image and how to create the right one for you! I am going to cover reputation and how to manage it, specifically in a digital age. But before I do, what on earth do you look like?

DRESS TO IMPRESS

> 'Clothes make the man. Naked people have little or no influence on society.'
>
> **Mark Twain**

Have you ever heard the expression 'Dress for the job you want, not the job you have'? It basically means that if you dress like a successful executive, and act like a successful executive, when it comes to promotions you will be perceived as a potentially successful executive.

There is a psychology behind how clothing influences others and how you are perceived, and whilst I believe that this is largely true and needs consideration, I also believe in this day and age there is more room for personal expression and individuality.

Many years ago, in the early days of social media, I delivered a key-note to a room full of professionals on how to take advantage of social media. Because my audience was all suited and booted I had decided to mirror them and dress formally with a pinstriped suit and a tie, which was not my usual business attire.

It was after my presentation that I was approached by an audience member who complimented me on my content but said they were distracted all the way through my presentation by the way I was dressed. They explained that I was talking about this exciting new age of technology, social media and entrepreneurship, yet I was dressed like an accountant.

For this simple reason alone I appeared less authentic . . . and she was right. It is not how I dress, ever. I had compromised my authenticity based on what I thought my audience would find more acceptable, and in doing so lost some of my authority on my subject.

Later I took that too far the other way, when talking to my speaker agent they were concerned that I was too casual and it was putting off the corporate audience.

You see, how you dress has a big impact on how people view you and, of course, how you feel about yourself.

One of my closest friends works in the field of wealth management and meets most of his clients in their own homes. These are all high net worth people.

When dealing with the affluent there is a fine line between looking successful and looking too successful. If you were to pull up in a better car than your customers, it may be perceived that your fees are too high, or indeed the opposite that you obviously know what you are doing.

After years in the industry, Matt dresses intentionally: a nice watch, a tailored suit and a quality shirt all reassure the client. But about five years ago he decided to stop wearing a tie, which was the historical norm and expectation in his industry.

Believe it or not he gave this decision a lot of consideration, he even asked me my opinion about it. After five years, he believes it has made a difference, but not in the way you might expect.

In five years not a single client mentioned the fact that he wasn't wearing a tie . . . until two weeks ago at the time of writing. Matt believes his clients have been more relaxed around him because he has been more relaxed, which underlines the point that how you dress has an impact on how you feel. I certainly remember the day I started to wear tailored suits and jackets and what that did to my confidence.

The important factor here is that Matt is still dressing congruent to his profession and the expectations of his customers. If he turned up in flip flops and a pair of shorts I am sure he would have less success.

Conversely, if you are looking to progress in a career at Google, a pinstripe suit will probably do you more harm than good.

Studies show, without doubt, that what you choose to wear to work impacts on how people perceive you; but more importantly it also impacts the way you feel about yourself.

In one study published in the *Journal of Applied Psychology* it was concluded that our self-perception changes to the extent that it alters our language too. The study demonstrated that participants dressed in more formal attire, described themselves using more formal adjectives. And the opposite was true of the more casually dressed participants.

Regardless of your style, colour will be noticed first and can play a big part in how we are perceived. Although this isn't an exact science, the cognitive effects triggered by colour will also apply to what you wear.

For example, wearing blue will have a calming effect; and studies have shown it can positively affect the creativity of your colleagues. Whereas red universally means stop, excitement or danger. Studies have shown red can also scare people or cause worry and distraction.

Darker tones are thought to be more authoritative and inspire confidence that you are capable, whereas lighter tones create the perception of being friendly or more gentle, certainly less intimidating.

My take on all of this is that it is far more important on your way up than it is once you arrive – and consistency is key. Take Steve Jobs for example. If you Google 'young Steve Jobs' you will see suits, shirts and ties. But as an older man, having achieved great things, he practically lived in jeans. Great leaders are not shy, they are not afraid to stand out and dress with confidence.

We meet a variety of different people every day and experience many complex interactions. The question to ask yourself is: do you believe the way you dress can positively impact the outcome or play to your advantage? I would argue a resounding 'yes' and encourage you to consider your day and dress accordingly.

So ask yourself:

- What do the influential people in your industry wear?
- What do your customers expect you to wear?
- What impression are you looking to make?

Then consider this:

- Perception is reality.
- Quality is always noticed.

A Moment of Reflection

- Have you ever given serious thought to the image you portray?
- What style would you like to be known for?
- Think about your target audience . . . what do you think they expect/accept?
- Think about the influencers in your industry, how do they present themselves?

Remember, for the accompanying strategy template and other resources go to www.InfluenceTheBook.com.

COLOURS THAT INFLUENCE

When it comes to branding, the psychology of colour is often debated. When you think of Virgin, what colour pops into your head? How about Facebook or LinkedIn?

We all have our own opinions about colour. For example, we choose colours for our clothing and when decorating our homes. But this chapter is not about choosing colours to highlight your skin tone as per the previous section on clothing. It's about choosing the right colours to reflect your brand values.

Colour is all around us and is a valuable source of information. It creates impact, it can reassure, it can sell, it can serve as a warning. It is said that people make up their minds within 90 seconds of being exposed to a person or a brand, and 62–90% of their assessment is based on colour alone.

According to a study by the University of Loyola, Maryland, colour increases brand recognition by up to 80%, and there is no reason why this should only benefit big brands, it can be used for personal branding too.

Prudent use of colours will contribute to influencing moods and feelings – positivity or negativity, calm or danger and so on – so therefore can influence attitudes.

When it comes to personal brand, it sits right alongside what font you use, what images you use and, of course, your logo. Why? Simply put, we are visual creatures who are emotionally stimulated by colour.

Your personal brand can be used in your absence – think about your website, your social profiles and your communications. Developing a strategy for using colour on all your communications will make you become more memorable and stand out from your competitors. By the way, I suggest just picking one or two; unless you have Google's marketing budget, establishing a four colour brand could prove difficult.

There are some things to think about when it comes to colour selection. I believe there are many misconceptions around the psychology of colour. We all have personal preferences, individual experiences, social conditioning and even cultural influences when it comes to colour. So to suggest that we are all going to react in exactly the same way is about as accurate as your daily horoscope.

However, we can perhaps accept there are some general patterns, and that a colour choice needs to be appropriate for a product or service. By appropriate I mean congruent. For example, let's accept for the sake of argument that red evokes urgency, excitement and energy. But on the flipside also danger. One might argue this wouldn't be the best brand decision for a firm of accountants. It is not a coincidence that more accountants choose blue (trust, security and dependability) than any other colour.

Predicting the reaction of your audience, and how appropriate they feel your colour choice is to your product or service, is important. Develop your strategy for how you will use colour as a personal branding tool. First, identify the colour that best reflects your brand. That doesn't necessarily mean you should choose your favourite colour, although that may be a good place to start. You need to understand that colours have meanings. It would be wise to consider those meanings before you determine if your favourite colour will be your customers' preference also.

Also be sure to look at your competitors. If everyone in your industry uses blue, use something else so that you stand out and are differentiated. Be mindful to choose a colour that conveys your authentic brand values and attributes.

Maybe the colour chart in Figure 3.1 will be useful when designing your personal brand. (For print readers, a full-colour version of this image is available at www.InfluenceTheBook.com.)

Of course, when you're communicating on behalf of your brand, you should use your brand colour consistently. Identify the PMS and HEX values (for printed materials, use PMS; and for your colour

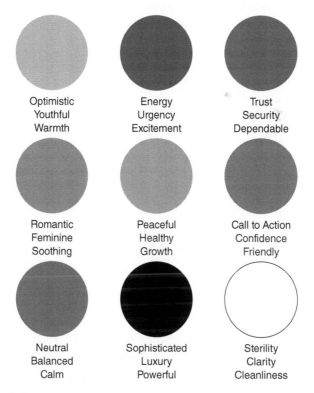

Optimistic	Energy	Trust
Youthful	Urgency	Security
Warmth	Excitement	Dependable

Romantic	Peaceful	Call to Action
Feminine	Healthy	Confidence
Soothing	Growth	Friendly

Neutral	Sophisticated	Sterility
Balanced	Luxury	Clarity
Calm	Powerful	Cleanliness

Figure 3.1

to appear correctly on the web, use web safe HEX). Your designer will be able to help, and Adobe Illustrator, Photoshop and InDesign have built-in conversions.

Here are some ideas for using colour for your personal brand:

- Use it on your website or blog.
- If a career professional, use it in your CV.
- Use it on your business cards and stationery.
- When developing presentations, use it on your slides.
- Include it on your social media profiles (banners, backgrounds etc.).
- Make it the background colour for your headshot photo on your online profiles (LinkedIn, Twitter, Quora etc.).
- Use it in your content (infographics, charts and imagery).
- Use it on your YouTube channel (YouTube lets you choose your palette).
- Use it in your videos as a background colour for the intro and outro.
- Use it on the cover of your proposals, bios, etc.
- Choose business accessories in your colour (iPad cover, briefcase, laptop bag, folders, etc.).
- Include in your email signature.
- Use coloured envelopes.
- Consider the promotional items you give away: mugs, t-shirts etc. (when selecting promo items, remember top of desk means front of mind).
- Incorporate your personal brand colours in what you wear (clothes and accessories).
- Brighten up your office with your brand colours (posters, artwork, desk accessories, screensaver, furniture etc.).

Colour usage can be powerful because it exudes brand attributes and makes you memorable.

A Moment of Reflection

- What colours would best serve your audience?
- Compare what you do now to the list above.
- Who do you know in your network that has already developed a personal brand? How do they apply colour?

Remember, for the accompanying strategy template and other resources go to www.InfluenceTheBook.com.

REPUTATION MATTERS

How others perceive us:

> *'Everywhere I go I'm second to arrive. My reputation precedes me.'*
>
> **Jarod Kintz**

Your reputation is simply how others perceive you, it is something you don't own. It is something you cannot control, only influence, and yet it remains one of your most valuable assets.

Reputation matters to even the most self-assured in society for very practical reasons – primarily money and relationships. It is hard to make a living if you are known as lazy and unreliable; it's hard to make friends if you are considered arrogant and grumpy; and it is hard to find a partner if you are thought to be a philanderer.

So, consider your reputation an instrument of convenience, which essentially makes your life easier or more difficult. A good reputation opens doors or attracts support, whereas a bad one creates obstacles and causes those same doors to slam in your face.

A reputation is also very fragile and can take years to build . . . but moments to destroy.

Several years ago, one of my members ran a charity dedicated to stopping bullying in the workplace. A very noble cause indeed; and motivated by her own personal experiences she tried to help organisations reduce bullying and provide individual victims with the support they needed.

Her reputation was excellent but, like all reputations, fragile. In 2010 the UK Prime Minister at the time, Gordon Brown, was accused of bullying staff in a book serialised in the *Observer*, a national newspaper.

Gordon Brown was defended at the time by senior Labour party member Lord Mandelson, who publicly claimed that no bullying was going on at No. 10.

The woman running the anti-bullying charity was asked by the media to comment and made the very valid point that, regardless of whether the claims were right or wrong, when an organisation faces an allegation relating to staff they should follow due process, which at least means investigation.

To publicly deny the allegation immediately, without following due process, was simply the wrong thing to do when it came to employment and HR and the government should have known better and set an example.

From that moment on she was at the heart of the story with most media outlets wanting her perspective.

Well, one morning she woke, went downstairs and opened her front door to retrieve the milk from her doorstep only to be greeted by an army of reporters literally camped out in her front garden. It was unexpected and she was surprised. In the heat of the moment she made a mistake. One that would cost her dearly.

One reporter asked her if her national helpline had received calls from staff at Downing Street, and she made the mistake of answering yes. It was a mistake because it was a confidential helpline and in no circumstances should she have broken confidence.

Understand she didn't say who or even what was discussed . . . she just said yes.

Well this was enough for people to be outraged and, I feel, she was quite unfairly demonised in the press. Even worse, suddenly everyone was reporting it. Now in this example the charity didn't have the largest footprint online, so if you were to type the charity into Google, all you would see was bad news. Years of good work down the drain and a reputation destroyed overnight.

A good reputation, like this example, is much harder to build than to destroy, and it is even harder to rebuild.

> *'It takes 20 years to build a reputation and five minutes to ruin it. If you think about that, you'll do things differently.'*
>
> **Warren Buffett**

But the biggest secret to building a great reputation is simply to become a person that deserves one. Practise the values and demonstrate the characteristics you want to be associated with on a daily basis. Avoid lip service and mouthing platitudes of great customer service and hard work. Live these values. Better still, let people discover them for themselves.

Below are just some of the benefits of a good reputation.

- Your reputation precedes you, which means you can open doors much faster and accelerate trust.
- A good reputation helps you to keep the bar high. We don't always feel deserving of a good reputation, but rather than

dwell on your weaknesses, why not let your reputation motivate you to be better?

- A good reputation gives you competitive advantage. You are easier to refer and recommend and can command what you are worth.
- A good reputation makes you an influencer. You become the role model that others look up to and attractive for media opportunities.
- A good reputation is a marketing strategy creating brand ambassadors out of customers.
- A good reputation opens the door to expansion and joint ventures.
- A good reputation helps you attract and retain customers.
- A good reputation helps you attract new talent.
- A good reputation helps you combat negative influences. It's like having an army of defenders in your network rise to your defence even when you are not there.

Caring about your reputation doesn't make you vain or self-obsessed. It doesn't make you insecure, requiring the approval of others. It simply means recognising that most will judge a book by its cover and, as long as our focus is on the substance of the read, why not have a cover that does justice to the content?

A Moment of Reflection

- If you were to ask your network what your reputation was, what do you think they would say?
- Identify three trusted colleagues, customers or contacts and ask them!
- What traits would you like to be known for?
- What could you do differently right now to start building the reputation you desire?

Remember, for the accompanying strategy template and other resources go to www.InfluenceTheBook.com.

YOUR IMAGE ONLINE

Front page of Google or nothing

> *'If it isn't on Google, it doesn't exist.'*
>
> **Jimmy Wales**

Q: Where is the best place to hide a dead body?
A: On the 3rd page of Google.

A major change over the last 25 years is our reliance on search engines for information and resources. People have the enormous advantage of information at their fingertips with thousands of search results in under a second. But it is often hard to tell what information is true and what is false.

As a result, we have become more sceptical, more resourceful and more reliant on sites/tools which corroborate information or, in the case of people, their reputation (which I will go into in more detail soon).

Building your influence will definitely have to include a strategy for your online presence and, ultimately, aiming for that number one spot in search engine results. Because of course we want to be visible to all who may need our products or services.

Google is the number one search engine in the world with over 100 billion searches every month, and 75% of the US market and over 90% of the global market. Focusing your efforts on Google is no bad idea but – worth noting if you intend to raise your influence in some other countries – it may not always be the best option. For example, in China, only around 11% of searches use Google.

If you are in business, it is important to realise that 93% of buying decisions start with an online search and therefore it's even more important to achieve page one when you consider the following.

- First page websites get 91.5% of all Google traffic.
- Page two receives 4.8% of traffic.
- Page three receives 1.1% only.

Even better still, the top spot on page one gets you an average share of 32.5% of the traffic, number two 17.6% and number three 11.4%.

It is important to know the difference between Search Engine Optimisation (SEO) vs Search Engine Marketing (SEM). They are frequently confused and used interchangeably but, essentially, SEO is the work you do on your site to ensure search engines like Google can find it (i.e. best practice) and SEM is promoting your website through search engines (typically paid advertising).

Paying for search engine results may not be for everyone, it all comes down to knowing your metrics and how well your site converts once you have the traffic.

A client of mine invests £500 a day on SEM, which they know will produce on average 11 very qualified leads. They convert 40% of their leads to customers and that is more than enough to turn a profit. Because they know their metrics and they have experimented, they know that increasing the SEM spend won't necessarily increase the qualified leads as theirs is a specialist service.

Google right now makes 500 algorithm changes per year with the intent of improving the search experience for end users. Whilst it is important to focus on keywords, relevancy etc., please keep front of mind the following with regards to your site.

1. **Satisfy intent**   Google now also monitors the second click when a user hits your site, not just the keyword that got you the click in the first place. Make sure the experience they have when they click is congruent with what they were looking for.

2. **Keywords are important, but less so than they used to be**   Google is now much better at interpreting meaning from your copy too and can assess if the copy on the page is a match to your headlines.

3. **Content is king**   Actually the user experience is king, but that comes from compelling and relevant content. Longer articles (1000 words plus) are preferred, but remember to build the page so that you keep attention. Also, unique images will be advantageous rather than overused stock images.

4. **Be mobile responsive**   Over 50% of Google searches come from mobile devices so make sure your site is mobile responsive or you may be penalised. Actually you should do this also because your audience will vote with their feet should the site be difficult to read.

Controlling the narrative

'Your brand isn't what you say it is, it's what Google says it is.'

Chris Anderson

So, having discussed the value of a good reputation above, what happens when bad news appears online? Anyone can create a site or page that disparages you and that's certainly not what you want employers or potential customers to find when they Google you.

It is time to take a proactive approach to getting your name out there and controlling your own narrative. Ordinarily the firms that manage this sort of thing for you can be quite costly, so below I've set out a few ideas.

Monitor Your Online Reputation

Google's own tool for tracking what it knows about a topic is Google Alerts. It is free to subscribe to and you can set up multiple alerts based on the keywords you want to use (your name or company name for example).

As soon as content matching your keywords enters Google's index, you are notified with a link via email. Do be warned that common phrases or key words will generate a lot of email.

Search Yourself

Perform a Google search for your name and company name. Repeat the same search for your name in Google Images too. It is worth checking several pages to see what is there.

Purchase Your Domain Name

Domains aren't expensive, but you will struggle with availability if you have a common name. If your name isn't available as a dot. com try variations which will help you get found, for example johnsmithspeaker.com.

Once you have the domain, build a personal website. There is more advice around blogging later in this book. Next, fill it with content focused on the topic you want to be found for.

Be Responsive

Now you are monitoring what is being said about you online, you may come across something which is false, inaccurate or simply paints you in a poor light. Using your blog, address the points you found and maintain control of the narrative. Google really likes fresh content, the more you update your site the more you will climb the ranks.

Additionally, your alerts may highlight articles where you have an opinion or can add value. Get stuck in and join the conversation. In responding to an alert where a negative comment has been made, don't shy away, but take the high road. It is easy to get sucked into an online spat; trust me, I have done it myself. But keep your discipline, be polite and remember you are representing your personal brand.

Increase Activity on Social Networks

A common excuse for not engaging with social media is lack of time. But I am assuming that because you are reading a book on influence, you understand the important role social media plays in communication today. Notice I didn't say join social networks in the title of this section . . . I said increase activity.

If you are adamant you don't have time, complete the profiles anyway, social platforms are typically high authority sites optimised for search engines. As a minimum consider Facebook, LinkedIn, Twitter and Google+. Also consider YouTube, Tumblr, Pinterest and Instagram.

You don't have to be a daily user, but try not to be totally inactive either. Use these channels to share your blog content or share the content of other influencers and start a dialogue with them.

> *On most of these sites you have options to optimise your profiles and even customise your URL. For example, on LinkedIn you can change your URL from a random string of characters to your name. Mine, for instance, is LinkedIn.com/in/WarrenCass (feel free to connect with me). Be sure to use your name and not a nickname if possible and use all of the options to connect your various accounts to each other.*

Be Careful What You Post

Remember to select your privacy settings carefully when posting content you don't want the world to see. Remember the Warren Buffett quote earlier in this book, a 20-year earned reputation can be destroyed overnight so apply your professional filter, i.e. your common sense.

If you are tagged in unflattering photos by others, you can remove unwanted tags.

Some favour managing two profiles – one for personal use and one professional. If you feel this is manageable then go for it. Lastly though, keep on top of the changes to privacy settings that social sites make with great regularity.

As a rule of thumb, assume nothing is truly private.

Images Matter More Than Ever

Remember to include images in your content strategy. The rise of image sites like Pinterest and Instagram have put the spotlight on the images that represent your brand. Most social sites favour images and video on their feeds, and they certainly receive plenty of engagement from users. Remember to select images carefully – those you think are reflective of your brand.

Everyone Loves a Review

It is not just restaurants that are under scrutiny from review sites. There are more and more digital review sites popping up all over the place and they are becoming much more vertical-specific. Whether you are a person or a business, reviews will become increasingly more important for you . . . reviews of your content, your book, your services etc. Think about strategies to get your raving fans engaged and supportive.

Authority Sites

This crosses over with a section in Chapter 5, Demonstrating Expertise, but be aware there are several types of authority sites which can help you build influence online.

Sites like Klout, PeerIndex and Kred measure your social influence with a whole bunch of complex algorithms which essentially determine the strength of your network, how engaged they are with your content, how influential they are in turn etc.

For me, these sites are more a measure of activity than anything else, so the key to ranking higher is to get more engaged, and have strategies to grow your network, particularly with other active influencers.

A Moment of Reflection

- Take a break and Google yourself! Dig deep to at least page 10. Include your company name. Where do you come on results?
- Set up some Google Alerts to keep you informed of any web content which mentions you or your business.
- What social media sites are you active on?
- What social media sites used by your market are you not active on?
- Browse your website with your mobile phone. How easy is it to use?

Remember, for the accompanying strategy template and other resources go to www.InfluenceTheBook.com.

THE IMPORTANCE OF SOCIAL PROOF

> *'Nothing influences people more than a recommendation from a trusted friend.'*
>
> **Mark Zuckerberg**

Enlightened influencers understand that social proof, or informational social influence, is a powerful tactic for easing the concerns of a worried consumer.

Social proof can lead large groups to conform to choices which are not always right, and is sometimes referred to as 'herd behaviour'. It is driven by the assumption that your peers possess more knowledge about a situation, person, product or service than you do.

According to research, over 70% of consumers read product reviews before they purchase and a review is 12 times more trusted than marketing literature; and 63% of consumers are more likely to use a site if it contains ratings and reviews.

Needless to say, if you are looking to grow your influence, it is in your best interests to effectively use social proof – and I will be covering this in much more detail throughout the book.

Marketers have always used social proof and we have always listened to the recommendations of friends and colleagues. For example, have you ever walked past a night club or a bar with a large line of people wanting to get in? This creates a perception of popularity intended to entice you to join the queue.

Or have you ever heard canned laughter on a TV show? Well, laughter is contagious and the purpose of the laughter track is to make you laugh more.

You may have seen many brands over the years that have used a slogan like '10,000 customers can't be wrong!' with the sole purpose of putting your mind at ease by thinking there is safety in numbers.

Think about the last time you needed the services of a tradesman like a builder or plumber. Would you take a chance on a name in the *Yellow Pages* (pre-internet of course)? Or would you be more likely to trust a referral from a friend who had received a good first-hand experience of a service?

Although, as a concept, social proof is nothing new, the game has changed thanks to social media; and user generated content online has made it much easier for marketers to take advantage of.

You can check a restaurant or hotel on TripAdvisor, or a builder on CheckaTrade.com – even an item on Amazon can be reviewed by customers all over the world. It is so much easier to research your purchases before you make them, giving you peace of mind.

I am going to share with you the five types of social proof. I'm going to tell you why they work and give some examples. Lastly, I will share how others may measure this in relation to your personal influence/brand.

1. Expert social proof

Expert social proof is endorsement from a credible, known expert and can come in several forms, including a press quote, a presentation, an article or blog they have written – or even a simple tweet.

When we as consumers want to buy something we are unfamiliar with, we will often seek expert opinion to become more confident in our decision.

Think about the business books you read (including this one) that have quotes from known authors or business leaders. This creates the perception 'If they think it's good, it must be worth buying!'

A known expert is arguably already considered an influencer and it has become a fairly common practice for brands to attract influencers to endorse them. This is referred to as 'influencer marketing' and is based on the principle of credibility by association.

If an influencer already has a positive reputation, then anything else they are involved with is seen more positively by association.

For example, at the height of BlackBerry's success they decided to run an influencer campaign reaching small business owners in the UK across several industry sectors. I was one of many people invited to participate – along with prominent speakers, authors and industry experts – where our image and case study explained to readers how we used our devices.

Another example is the Hawaiian Tourism Department who collaborated with popular travel Instagramers who were known to visit beautiful destinations around the world. They posted amazing images with the hashtag #LetHawaiiHappen and generated over 100,000 posts reaching 54% of travellers across the USA.

2. Celebrity social proof

This is similar to expert social proof, but the endorsement comes from a celebrity instead. Celebrities are really good for drawing attention, and providing we have a positive view of the celebrity, i.e. want to be like them, we will be more inclined to mimic their behaviour or choices.

A great example of this is Facebook founder Mark Zuckerberg who shared the fact that he was using the iGrill, a cooking thermometer with an app that integrates with Facebook. iGrill didn't even know he was a customer until he posted something positive about it online, resulting in their website crashing with over 1000 visitors entering the site every minute.

Another great example was the infamous celebrity-filled group selfie taken at the Oscars by Bradley Cooper and tweeted by Ellen DeGeneres. This one photo alone was thought to be worth $800 million to $1 billion to Samsung who sponsored the event (the device used for the photo was also by Samsung).

The tweet itself was retweeted over 3 million times in just two days and you couldn't even see the brand of phone used. But 43 million viewers watched on TV with the brand clearly on display.

3. User social proof

User social proof is approval from existing customers and can include case studies, testimonials and online reviews. The latter being the main focus of sites like TripAdvisor and Yelp and really important to users of eBay and Amazon.

Because we are deeply empathetic creatures we tend to imagine ourselves in other people's shoes when we read their reviews or hear their stories. Because stories tend to evoke emotions, they stay with us.

A study conducted by BrightLocal found that 88% of consumers read online customer reviews and that 85% read up to 10 reviews before they feel they can trust a business.

So what do your customer reviews say about you? Do you even collect testimonials? Most of us will have a LinkedIn profile, but does your network endorse you? Have you asked them to?

When you receive good testimonials, consider how you share these with the world. Definitely make sure you add them to your website. Also, wherever possible, use pictures. Not only do we know that people like looking at human faces on the web, we know they are much more likely to trust the testimonial. Help yourself by choosing a smiling friendly photo and including your call to action. Prominent client logos are also highly memorable.

4. 'Wisdom of the crowds' social proof

The key to this type of social proof is demonstrating that thousands or millions have already taken the decision to go with you. Safety in numbers as it were.

There is also the fear of missing out (FOMO) often ridiculed in popular culture but, let me tell you, this is a very real thing and a form of social anxiety particularly prevalent on social media where people constantly compare their daily lives to those of their peers.

This is a particularly powerful technique when used to share 'People who bought this also bought that' (think Amazon), or sites that list best sellers like iTunes. Have you ever been persuaded to buy a book or song because it sat on a best-seller list?

5. 'Wisdom of your friends' social proof

Sites like Facebook have really used this to great effect to spark engagement. When presented with a sponsored page or post, we can see which of our friends and family have liked and shared it and are far more likely to gravitate towards them.

In fact, 77% of consumers say that word-of-mouth feedback from family and friends is their most persuasive deciding factor when making purchasing decisions.

This relates to the hypothesis of 'implicit egotism' which is the idea that humans have an unconscious preference for things, people and places that they associate with or resemble. For example, we will strongly prefer the letters in our name or the numbers in our date of birth.

Studies show we value the opinions we perceive as most like ours, or tend to favour articles that support our existing point of view, otherwise known as confirmation bias.

Because most people will befriend others who have things in common with them, it makes perfect sense that referral programmes are successful – or indeed the 'Like' button on a Facebook page.

So to summarise this chapter: technology has made it easier to share good news (and bad), but keep your message punchy because it is so much harder to get and keep attention. Lastly, remember the internet has a long memory and people care about what others say about you, so manage your reputation carefully and actively encourage your customers to leave a testimonial.

A Moment of Reflection

- How many testimonials do you have on LinkedIn?
- How could you increase this number?
- What review sites are relevant to you and your industry?
- Do you display testimonials and case studies on your website? If not, why not?
- Who are your best customers who might be willing right now to write a great testimonial for you?

Remember, for the accompanying strategy template and other resources go to www.InfluenceTheBook.com.

4

C IS FOR COMMUNICATION

In 1918, a chap by the name of Charles Riborg Mann published his findings from a study in engineering education. He concluded that success in this field was in fact not down to technical knowledge or skills, but was a result of the ability to communicate effectively.

Following his findings, Harvard University, Stanford Research and the Carnegie Foundation conducted further research and they concluded that 85% of career success is a result of well-developed people skills and only 15% is down to knowledge or technical skills.

This effectively means that it doesn't really matter how ambitious you are, how much commitment you show or how educated you are, if your communication skills are poor, you will still have a low probability of success.

I am not saying that intelligence is overrated, just that your IQ (Intelligence Quotient) is less significant than your emotional intelligence and moral intelligence scores when it comes to predicting success.

Let me put it even more simply: your ability to communicate on a human level is the key to your success.

Effective communication can improve all of your key relationships – from colleagues to family and friends. It is fundamental for connection and trust building, it improves team building and decision making and helps you avoid the frustration of not being understood.

> *'The quality of your life is the quality of your communication.'*
>
> **Tony Robbins**

The good news is that everyone can develop their communication skills; and I believe that even the smallest improvement in your ability to make a connection with others will make a profound difference.

In this section of the book I want to help you become more aware of how you come across to others, and I will share some ideas on how to become more influential in your day-to-day interactions.

Most of us communicate instinctively. We don't overthink what we are going to say or indeed how we say it. But effective communication is about more than just talking, we also send messages out through our body language and our micro expressions, which will reinforce or contradict the words we say. Our ability to listen effectively, empathise and make considered responses often determines our success.

Let's start with some self-awareness. Take a moment to consider the following questions and be honest with yourself. Give yourself a score out of 10.

A Moment of Reflection

How effective a communicator are you under pressure?
Do you panic? Do you stress other people out? Do you miss the social nuances which achieve a better response from others?

How good a team player are you? Do you play well with others or prefer to work more independently?

What are your negotiation skills like? Do you typically create win–win situations or do you cut off your nose to spite your face?

How good are you at developing other people? Do you mentor/coach your staff, colleagues or children?

Are you personally accountable? Do you accept responsibility when you make mistakes or are you too proud to acknowledge your failings?

How self-aware are you? Do you know how you are perceived by others? How do you think they would describe you? Does this match the impression you want to make?

Do you think your physical state affects your communication? Do you take your moods to work with you? Do you act differently when tired, hungry or stressed? How does this impact others?

How did you score yourself? I would imagine the vast majority of us have room for improvement, yet most will typically favour the hard skills over the soft when it comes to investing time and money on training and development. Remember the 100-year-old lesson, perhaps the emphasis should be proportional to the impact with 85% of our focus on soft skills?

Remember, for the accompanying strategy template and other resources go to www.InfluenceTheBook.com.

EFFECTIVE COMMUNICATION STARTS WITH GOOD INTUITION

Intuition, sometimes referred to as your inner guide, is your ability to instinctively understand something without the need for conscious reasoning. It is the inner voice that we all have (to varying degrees), and the good news is it can be developed to make us more effective communicators.

You will have heard it referred to as 'following a hunch' or 'trusting your gut', but it can be powerfully harnessed when talking to others and you simply need to learn to trust it.

It starts with good observation. In a previous chapter I encouraged you to become a student of people, which is effectively having a better understanding of others' personality and communication styles so you can adapt how you speak to the way they best receive information. After running over a thousand networking events, I can tell you with great confidence that a minority of people do this well, yet some people do it instinctively and unconsciously.

Have you ever been in the middle of a conversation when your gut was telling you the other person just wasn't interested or was distracted? Essentially your subconscious mind was picking up on their verbal and non-verbal clues, helping you to become more aware of the reality of the situation. When you became aware, what did you change?

Learn to trust what your gut is telling you! If something doesn't feel quite right, the chances are it isn't. Have you ever had a feeling in the pit of your stomach telling you to do something and you ignored it? Only to regret it later? Especially when it comes to effective communication, you need to trust your intuition and allow it to guide you.

All I am suggesting here is that you PAY ATTENTION and be aware. In order to improve your intuitive ability, you must pay attention to your surroundings. The more information you absorb from your environment, the better your decision making will be. This is equally true when speaking to a group or to an individual. What clues are they giving you as to their level of interest? Are they looking at their watch or over your shoulder for something more interesting? Or are they making good eye contact and asking lots of questions?

IT'S NOT WHAT YOU SAY IT'S HOW YOU SAY IT

You may have heard this phrase before, personally I don't entirely buy it and I will come back to explain why shortly. In the meantime, however, there is some truth to it.

Imagine you are a buyer or potential customer and Gavin the salesperson turns up to present to you. Gavin is visibly nervous as he shuffles into the room with his shoulders dropped and his head down, not a single bit of eye contact is made.

Gavin's suit is crumpled where he wore the jacket in the car and his shirt looks like it could do with an iron. He coughs to clear his throat then starts to speak in a monotone timid voice, 'Good afternoon everyone, my name is Gavin and I am going to spend the next 15 minutes telling you about our product and how it can help you.'

Not a great first impression. But hey, you are probably a really nice person and give Gavin a chance anyway. But imagine if he had done the opposite . . .

Salesperson Gavin strides into the room with his head held high, his shoulders back and a beaming smile on his face. He immediately, respectfully and confidently says, 'Good afternoon everyone' making eye contact with each person in turn.

His suit is tailored and he looks well-groomed and professional. Making eye contact again, he starts to speak in a clear, confident voice. 'My name is Gavin and I am going to spend the next 15 minutes telling you about our product and how it can help you.'

I don't know if you spotted it, but the *words* Gavin spoke were exactly the same in both scenarios. It was the way he said it that was different, as was the impression he made from his confidence and appearance.

There is even research which suggests we are more likely to believe a poor argument when delivered in a confident manner, than we are a logical argument presented by someone showing self-doubt. Think about it, have you ever been on a quiz team where one member is utterly convinced of the answer but is wrong? Someone else on the team had the correct answer but maybe wasn't sure, so you selected the incorrect answer.

There is no denying the importance of a well-delivered message. Tone of voice, congruence with body language – even the setting – all have an impact on how the message is received. So here are a few ideas to help you improve your non-verbal communication.

Show genuine interest

Give listeners the impression you are enthusiastic about talking to them. People love to feel important, and you can make this happen by making them feel that you would rather be talking to them than anyone else at that precise moment. When you make them feel better about themselves, they are far more likely to open up to you.

Simple visual clues will demonstrate your interest to them, like nodding your head, making eye contact and of course the universal facial expression for 'interested'. What, you haven't heard of this? You can do it with me now if you like: bunch your eyebrows towards the top of your nose, tilt your head slightly to one side, imagine making eye contact and very slowly nod your head. Easy, huh? Remember to react also to what they say, if they make a joke and you maintain that expression it might get awkward.

Listen well

Try not to focus too much on what you want to say next as they speak. Instead, listen attentively to their words and respond as relevantly as you can. This will demonstrate you are engaged and interested in what they are saying.

Listen to all opinions and encourage everyone to speak up, especially those who usually keep their opinions to themselves. Show that you respect what they are saying and that they are valued. This in turn will create an atmosphere of mutual trust, respect and teamwork.

Truth be told, people are really interested in themselves first. By being interested in them, they will naturally like you more. You can still lead the conversation, just make sure it stays about them, which will make them feel like they are in charge.

For example, let's say you are at a networking event talking to a new contact and they mention a recent holiday. You can base your questions on this: Where did you go? Was it activity based or relaxing? Who did they go with? All of your questions lead to answers, which in turn can lead to more questions.

The more open-ended your questions are, the more likely it is that you will gain insight into their wants and needs and be able to offer fresh new perspectives about their situation. This will deepen your connection and make them feel heard.

A couple of years ago I was in conversation with a friend of mine who runs her own hairdressing salon. In the main she was really happy with her team who had been with her for years and all were good at their jobs. However, some consistently received more tips than others, and this was starting to cause friction as the company policy was to share all tips evenly amongst staff.

Upon investigation the only difference between those receiving the larger tips and those receiving small or no tips at all was: the top performers got the customers talking about themselves.

She told me the moment they realised this, they were able to train their team to be more inquisitive about their clients and show genuine interest. Sure enough, very soon everyone's tips increased, even the top performers improved because they were now aware of the reason and were asking better questions.

Be social

What do I mean by this? Well, in a business context, I have observed that most first-time interactions tend to be a little formal. People talk about work or their business without trying to connect on a human level.

In the past, when we ran networking events, we would let people arrive and mingle for a period of time before interrupting them and introducing an icebreaker which got them speaking about non-work related things, such as hobbies and interests, family and pets, achievements and charitable activities. During this exercise you could hear the difference in the noise levels in the room, with people smiling more and laughing.

Our conclusion: you will build rapport so much quicker if you can get people talking about their passions rather than the usual small talk. In the UK we joke about talking about the weather to fill awkward silences; instead, ask someone what they did over the weekend and see where that leads.

Be mindful of your body language

Body language is a fairly big topic which has been written about extensively. It's a fascinating subject, and I recommend spending more time on it once you have mastered the basics both as a reader of other people's body language and a master of your own.

Here, I just want to share with you the basics to help you make more of an impact in your day-to-day encounters.

Body language is like a second conversation taking place in the background, we are often oblivious to it, and it is mainly only picked up on at a subconscious level.

Learning to control what your body is saying to support your words or demonstrate your interest is an essential part of influencing and, of course, being likeable.

First, make sure you *make good eye contact*, but in moderation as you don't want to appear too intense. Eye contact not only communicates you are interested, but it shows confidence and creates trust. As a result, people will naturally pay more attention to you and what you have to say.

Next, *smile*! Scientists and spiritual leaders alike are in total agreement that a simple smile can affect not only you, but the world around you too. Current research (and a dose of common sense) tells us that smiling is contagious.

When you smile at people you are effectively communicating to them that you like them, in the main they will naturally smile back which builds rapport. But your smile needs to be authentic or it will be noticed. Smile also from the eyes as if you are really happy to be meeting or speaking, it makes all the difference.

Smiling also has the added benefit of lifting our own mood, we have a physical reaction in the brain which releases neuropeptides, that work towards fighting stress, as well as dopamine, endorphins and serotonin. This is relaxing, lowering heart rates and blood pressure and lengthening lives.

Lastly, smiling actually makes you more attractive to others and they will treat you differently. You will appear more reliable, sincere and relaxed.

According to a study published in the journal *Neuropsychologia*, seeing a smiling face activates your orbitofrontal cortex, which is the region of your brain which processes sensory rewards. This explains the findings of the Face Research Laboratory at the University of Aberdeen in Scotland (2011) where subjects were asked to rate attractiveness. Both men and women were more attracted to the images of people smiling and, in particular, where eye contact was also made.

Try it. Next time you go out wear a huge smile and measure people's response. You will have the added bonus of feeling good.

Next, *look alert*, demonstrate your attentiveness and avoid looking distracted by something else. Focus yourself before you enter the room with a little self-talk or a coffee, whatever works for you.

Match their body language. You can always tell when someone has good rapport with you because you will find yourself mimicking each other naturally. But you can nudge the process along by subtly mimicking their posture or movements, which will make them feel more connected to you and they won't know why.

Just don't be too obvious when you practice mimicking, because if they realise what you are doing they will feel like they are being manipulated, which will have the opposite effect and make them defensive.

Display open body language, keeping your movements relaxed and deliberate; using open arm gestures shows you are less guarded with nothing to hide. Particularly when showing the palms of your hands.

People who use open gestures are perceived in a more positive light and are considered more persuasive than those who fold their arms, hide their hands or hold objects too close to their body. These are considered defensive poses, which breed mistrust.

Use your hands. Whilst on the subject of hands, brain imaging has shown that a region in the frontal lobe called Broca's area, which is associated with language, is also activated when we make gestures with our hands. So using gestures helps our ability to think!

Research has shown that when we use our hands our speech is less hesitant, our verbal content improves and filler words are reduced (you know, the 'ums' and 'errs' which occur while we fill time searching for the next sentence).

Have a play with this but don't overdo it. You don't want people to think they are in a game of charades, but you will find it improves your clarity and helps with your articulation.

Lastly with the hands: *your handshake*. Touch is the most powerful and primitive non-verbal cue. The right handshake will make you more credible and trustworthy, especially when coupled with a smile and good eye contact as above.

Be careful not to grip too hard or you will come across as a bully. Be careful not to be too limp, commonly known as the 'dead fish', as you will appear weak and pathetic. Be careful not to hold too long as you might come across as a psycho stalker, especially when coupled with an intense stare. ;-)

Next, we want to demonstrate we are really interested and that the person we are speaking to has our full attention. Your reminder for this is the nursery rhyme 'Head, shoulders, knees and toes, knees and toes'.

Let's start with the *head*.

If you want someone to see you agree with what they are saying, *nod your head*. This is sometimes used by salespeople to encourage agreement and is used just before or whilst asking a question where they want a positive response. You see when someone nods at us we unconsciously feel the need to nod back at them; as we have already discussed, we mimic when in rapport.

You can play with this as well: should they make a really interesting point, raise your eyebrows and smile while you nod, this again shows you to be really listening.

Do me a favour though, and try not to look like the nodding dog toy or a nodding Santa – don't overdo it. I once delivered a talk on body language just before the break at a conference. During the break everyone was networking and half the room was nodding, trying faithfully to apply what I had shared. It looked like an AC/DC concert, only in suits. Very funny though.

Next, the *shoulders*.

This one is simple: if you want to show someone you are interested in them, *lean in* slightly. Tilting your head and shoulders towards someone makes them feel listened to and important. We all like a bit of flattery don't we?

If they also lean, it shows you are in rapport. Just don't get too close as this will be seen as a threat.

Knees and toes, knees and toes.

Pointing your knees and feet towards someone is a positive signal. It shows you are interested. It can also be used to influence a decision (pointing to your favoured choice can influence unconsciously).

At a networking event, you can see which conversations to avoid by looking at their feet. Groups which are closed with shoulders square, leaning in and feet pointing towards each other are probably engrossed in a conversation and don't want to be interrupted. Whereas groups with feet pointing away from each other, standing at an angle, are more likely to be receptive to an interruption.

Equally, if you want to draw a conversation to an end, simply open up your shoulders and subtly pivot your feet away.

Next up: *THE POWER POSE!* Power and confidence can be displayed through our posture and our use of the space around us.

Taking a slightly wider stance can help us appear solid and grounded. Whilst keeping your upper body erect with your shoulders back and your head held high makes you look self-assured.

By standing, you will look more powerful than those seated around you. For the last 20 years I have had a golden rule: never sit in a reception area. If a client or prospect comes to collect me I will always be on my feet looking ready (besides, sitting just crumples up my suit and makes me look slouched). Remember this if you are going for an interview and all the other candidates are sitting down.

If you do happen to be seated, you can look more confident by simply placing both feet flat on the floor and widening your arms away from your body. Again, keep your upper body erect with your shoulders back.

If you really want to appear dominant you can go full superman – you know, with your hands on your hips and your chest sticking out – though I'm not sure where you would want to use this, if at all. Maybe if you are facing a confrontational meeting where you want to hold your ground. You can always tone it down with a wider stance, but with your arms by your sides.

Three quick things to avoid

Sighing   We sigh for many reasons including exhaustion, frustration, sadness and boredom. A sigh will typically leave someone wondering what's the matter with you; but if they don't know you well enough they probably won't ask.

Invading personal space   We all have a bubble of personal space around us which, when someone we don't know well enters uninvited, can trigger irritation or fear.

Over stare   When strangers stare at us too long it is often perceived as a threat and is also seen in the animal kingdom in apes and other social animals.

A Moment of Reflection

- Being honest with yourself, when you talk to others, how much are you focused on them?
- How do you mentally and physically prepare for a networking event? If you don't prepare, how do you think that affects your energy and the way you communicate?
- Think about the language you use. What negative words could you start to drop from your vocabulary right now?
- What do you think your body language says about you?

Remember, for the accompanying strategy template and other resources go to www.InfluenceTheBook.com.

Using our voices – voice tone

Using our vocal tones taps into the musical aspects of our voices. Let's explore this, as well as pitch, volume, emphasis and pace.

Research conducted by the University of Pittsburgh, USA, revealed that people make subconscious judgements about others based on their tone of voice. Specifically, perceiving people with deeper voices to have more authority, which is thought to be a throwback to a time when one's status was determined by one's strength and physical stature. Typically, bigger people were dominant and, typically, bigger people have deeper voices.

How does this help you? Well, all of us have a vocal range to a varying degree, and by using the lower end of your range, you will improve the impact of your message. Now I am not suggesting that we all go around doing Barry White impressions; stay comfortably within your range, just use the lower end.

Consider the opposite. When you hear a high pitched or shrill voice, how do you react on an emotional level? Again, according to the research, a high pitched voice is perceived to lack authority, and for many can be an irritation.

Don't take my word for this by the way. Think about the powerful characters in movies. Of course there are exceptions, but most powerful or authoritative characters are played by actors with deeper voices, think Darth Vader, or Sean Connery as James Bond.

Some are lucky to have a naturally warm, attractive voice quality. Think Richard Burton for example. There is an old-fashioned compliment to actors: 'I'd listen to them reading the phone book' which may have been first applied to Richard Burton. I forget the radio station, but I did hear him once do it, and let me tell you it was still captivating.

It is also important to vary your tone as opposed to speaking in a monotone. A varied tone will rise and fall and inject energy into your message. A monotone voice lacks range because it maintains a constant pitch; and it also lacks stress variety. This makes it harder for the listener to concentrate and focus on the message.

Think about the people you consider to be good verbal communicators. They probably have a certain dynamism to their voice and can convey emotion, enthusiasm and even humour simply by varying tone.

And lastly, SLOW DOWN. Speaking slower can have a positive impact on your authority for four main reasons.

Reason 1   You will appear more grounded, calm and collected in your thoughts. Take the time to centre yourself and proceed mindfully and deliberately. Life can often be really stressful, so when we encounter people who are laid back and calm, we are more attracted to them. There is something quite irresistible about those who know how to bring the intensity down a notch.

Reason 2   When you slow down your speech, you have more time to select the right words to express yourself meaningfully. Many people have sesquipedalian vocabularies (see what I did there?), but rarely use the words they know.

Reason 3   You will improve your articulation, giving you time to pronounce each syllable properly. We generally perceive people who both use a larger vocabulary and articulate well as more intelligent. Whether they are is a different discussion: it's perception that counts here.

Reason 4   This is, in my opinion, the most important of the four. It gives the listener time to digest the message. If you want people to take action from your message, there is a big difference between hearing and understanding. Hearing takes no effort at all, but understanding means focusing your mind on the meaning of what is being said. Using pauses will also help your ability to be understood.

ACTUALLY, IT'S ALSO WHAT YOU SAY . . . AND WHAT YOU DO!

'I am all for conversations, but you need to have a message.'

Renee Blodgett

How you say something is important, but I will now argue that what is being said, and what actions you take, are of equal or greater importance.

You may have heard of the 7% rule? I prefer to call it the 7% misrepresentation.

In 1971, a book was published called *Silent Messages* by Professor Albert Mehrabian which discusses the results of his research into non-verbal communication. In it, he concludes that in a sales situation our overall assessment of a salesperson's credibility is based on factors outside of the words they use – how they look and sound, for instance.

I reject this claim as a pernicious myth which has been used time and again by communication consultants, speaker trainers and coaches. In fact, I'm tired of hearing it, like the old adage 'The exception that proves the rule'. How can an exception prove a rule? Surely it's the opposite that is proved. I digress, but this one comes from old English where the meaning of the term 'prove' meant to test not to confirm. So really it should be 'The exception that tests the rule'.

What you say is more important than how you say it, style is NOT more important than substance. But that doesn't mean you should only concentrate on one of them!

I mean, think about it, human speech is amazing, we get so much information from it. When we listen to someone speaking, we can make a reasonably informed guess about their age, gender, their mood and where they grew up. Oh, and there are the words they say too!

Anyway, back to the 7% myth. So, firstly, this research had nothing to do with delivering speeches nor day-to-day conversation, it was based solely on the information that could be conveyed using a single word.

There were two studies. In the first, participants were asked to listen to a woman's voice speaking the word 'maybe' in three different ways to convey liking, disliking and neutrality. At the same time, they were shown pictures of her face conveying the same emotions. Participants were asked to identify the emotion with the spoken word, then with the picture and lastly with the two combined. It won't surprise you that the combined results were more accurate. If communication was only about words we would never have a need for emojis;-).

In the second study, participants listened to nine words, three meant to convey liking (thanks, dear and honey), three for disliking (don't, brute and terrible) and the last three neutral (oh, really and maybe). Each word was heard with three different pronunciations and participants were asked to identify the emotions being conveyed. Naturally, the tone of voice was a bigger influencer than the word itself.

The studies were combined to conclude the 7% rule, as participants weighted their guess on 55% body language, 38% tone of voice and 7% from the word.

Calling this a rule based on two studies is at best premature. In science, a rule is more robustly tested by multiple studies – so this does little for scientific integrity.

More importantly though I believe this is a misrepresentation of Mehrabian's own conclusion, which was that body language and tonality may be more accurate indicators when communication is inconsistent or contradictory. Obviously, with your communication, whether it be a speech, a meeting or day-to-day conversation, I would hope you never confuse by being inconsistent in what you say and how you say it.

So, now we have put that point to bed, let's have a look at what you say.

Share your vision and develop accountability

In fact, I am going to extend this section beyond ideas and include personal goals, objectives and ambitions.

Now there is a natural tendency by most to hold ideas very close to their chests through fear of them being stolen. People fear sharing goals through fear of not achieving them. People fear sharing ambitions through fear of ridicule or failing.

Notice the theme here: fear. Fear holds us back and stops us achieving, but it is time to share your intentions despite your natural fears; and here is why.

When you share your ideas, you create opportunities for feedback and collaboration, and you develop a sense of accountability. Many entrepreneurs tell me that the simple act of sharing an idea makes them more committed to it because of the above benefits, which more than outweigh the risk of them being stolen.

The fact is that we have ideas in abundance, but rarely do people have the discipline or the resources to make them happen. By sharing, you will find people with the time and skills, inspired by your vision, stepping forward to help.

The same is true when you share goals. Have you ever shared a desire to lose more weight or get fitter with friends only to have them ask how it's going weeks later? This too is accountability.

If you are working for a larger organisation, you will probably already have some form of accountability. However, those who work in isolation often don't have any at all. In my humble opinion, it is worth seeking it out either from a coach, a friend, a master-mind group (my personal favourite) or a mentor. Here are four good reasons to increase your accountability.

1. **Accountability improves performance** If you are anything like me, you have your moments where the slightest thing will distract you and send you off on a tangent. I have found accountability has made me more focused and reduced the time I spend on unproductive activities.

2. Accountability encourages ownership   With my own team, I have found that making individuals more accountable for their actions means they value their work more and feel more important to the company. Their roles are clearer and they are happy to take ownership.

3. Accountability builds trust   This is probably the most important benefit of accountability, because when people take ownership, they make commitments.

4. Accountability develops us   With the right support and feedback, accountability will develop the skills and confidence of you and your team.

Another benefit of sharing our ideas with others is that it tends to bring out our passion. Don't underestimate just how attractive someone talking with passion can be, it's like a magnet to positive people.

Ultimately though, you will never be considered a visionary leader or influencer if you keep your vision to yourself!

Avoid criticising

No one likes being around people who moan and whine about everything. I call them 'mood hoovers' because they suck the energy out of every room. I literally cannot be around them for very long because it starts to drain me and affect my own mood.

If you are a complainer and you are not careful it will have an impact on your personal relationships, your professional career will stall and even your own mental, emotional and physical health could suffer.

People have more respect for others who are constructive, those who present solutions and look to build people up rather than bring them down.

Now I am not saying you should never confront a problem if you come across it or provide feedback should it be necessary. You might just be more effective if you approach it constructively.

A study conducted by the US Army suggests that in order to take on board constructive criticism, people need to be praised eight times. This perhaps tells you what impact you are having on others if you are overcritical.

When people feel like they are being attacked their natural tendency is to become defensive. Since many consider the best form of defense is attack, you might just find they trigger the same response in you, and then it's all downhill from there.

I mention no names, but I have had two friends in the last 30 years where I felt it necessary to feedback their negativity to them. I approached both constructively and was able to share examples and how it was making others feel.

One of them was prepared to change and consciously started to amend her behaviour. It didn't happen overnight as it is a hard habit to change, but in time she transformed. Much later she shared what a difference it had made to her life. She was included in more social events through her work and was promoted fairly quickly. It improved her relationship with her own daughter, and she attributes the change in attitude as the reason she saved her marriage. Overall she felt healthier and happier, and was grateful for the feedback.

As for the other friend, I couldn't tell you what he is doing right now. He was reluctant to take the feedback on board and didn't change a single thing. In fact, he became even more of a victim and ultimately toxic to me, so we lost touch. Such a shame.

Be interested *and* interesting

We have previously discussed showing genuine interest, and you may have heard the saying 'Be interested, not interesting' in the context of networking. Dale Carnegie said it slightly differently: 'To be interesting, be interested.' Whilst I agree with this more, I am still not 100% onboard. Why not be interested *and* interesting at the same time?

People often talk about elevator pitches, which I have to say I dislike when they sound over-rehearsed and try to be too clever. Of course, we need to be able to articulate succinctly who we are and what we do, I am just encouraging you to make it intriguing. People asking you questions back is a good indicator that they are equally interested. Instead of delivering an elevator pitch, which robotically states who you are and what you do, why not share an example of a problem you have solved for your client/boss/colleague (insert noun of your choice)? This is even more effective if the example you give can be related to your conversation so far.

Story telling

Another great way to be interesting is to tell stories. Stories have enormous power to elicit a response from others – whether they are intended to inspire, enchant, educate, challenge or motivate. Painting pictures with your words so others can understand your message – engaging imaginations – might well be the most effective weapon in your armoury.

Most people have totally conformed to the sterile business-as-usual approach to communicating ideas. Using data and statistical analysis or death by PowerPoint. I even heard someone once say they had put together a PowerPoint presentation that even *they* wouldn't want to sit through. Why would you do this?

Let's face it, we are ALL experts in consuming stories. From the childhood stories our parents repeated to teach us our morality or inspire us to be more, to the stories told in TV advertising messages where big brands flog their wares. We have been doing it for thousands and thousands of years, as evidenced by prehistoric cave drawings.

Hollywood has taught us a whole heap of lessons too on how we can engage with people on an emotional level, yet we largely ignore this proven, tried-and-tested form of communication when it comes to our daily lives.

There is no doubt in my mind that the best leaders, speakers, teachers, mentors, trainers, writers, salespeople and even parents in the world are good at telling stories to get their message across.

I am sure you have heard of TED Talks (if not, have you been living under a rock somewhere?) where world-class speakers speak in simple narratives using powerful imagery to aid their story telling. Take some time to watch a few of these on YouTube and observe just how effective they are at making you feel what they are talking about.

When we tell our personal stories, we build an emotional connection with our audience. If it is self-deprecating they will consider us more honest and humble, if it includes the challenges we have faced they will feel empathy, and if we share injustice they will feel anger. The key word here is 'feel'. They won't just hear us; they will feel us.

There is not a person anywhere in the history of the world who has been motivated to take action when they have felt indifference. So make them feel something else!

So, what stories should you be telling in business? A good starting point for most professionals is their *why?* story. Why do you do what you do? If you want to persuade your audience, then use a 'purpose story' which conveys your ideas of the bigger picture. If you want to share how others have overcome the same problems, share 'proof stories'. Also, think cautionary tales, lessons from failures, examples of triumph over adversity. By including your everyday experiences, where appropriate of course, you will be considered more authentic, more relatable and trustworthy.

Here are my five tips for effective story telling.

1. When constructing your story, consider first **who is your audience** and **what do you hope to achieve** by telling the story?

2. Make it relatable, **talk about people**. We naturally like to compare ourselves to central characters so we can imagine what we would have done in the same circumstances. Let your characters speak for themselves with their unique identities. Quote them, it lends authenticity to the narrative. This is a great way to get people engaged.

3. **Connect emotionally**. We as humans are far more likely to take action when we care about something. Share how your characters feel. Include the bombshell moments, the obstacles and the injustices. Then share the highs of the victory moments and explain what they meant. Make your story worthy of their attention.

4. People have limited attention spans. So, **don't bore your audience**! Don't draw your story out for the sake of it; instead keep them in suspense wondering what will happen.

5. Lastly, **what is your moment of truth**? It should be clear to your audience when your story is over what the underlying message was. The significant lesson or *aha* moment. Make it a powerful idea worthy of sharing.

A Moment of Reflection

- Take a blank sheet of paper and list your stories. Consider the following.
  - Your victories and achievements.
  - Your failures and what you learned.
  - Your most embarrassing moments.
  - Your biggest coincidences.
  - The big injustices you have witnessed.
  - When justice was served.
  - Stories that touched your heart.
  - People that totally inspire you and why.
  - Stories which gave you a different appreciation of other cultures.
  - When you were lucky.
  - Your funny business stories.
- Think about how you can incorporate these stories into your marketing, blogs and talks.

Remember, for the accompanying strategy template and other resources go to www.InfluenceTheBook.com.

Build people up

'You need to be aware of what others are doing, applaud their efforts, acknowledge their successes, and encourage them in their pursuits. When we all help one another, everybody wins.'

Jim Stovall

In a while, I'll talk about using names, which is a powerful way to engage people. Building them up is another great way to make them feel good about themselves and they will associate this feeling with you.

We all like a genuine compliment. Receiving a sincere compliment can have a profound impact on our day and it doesn't need to be big, just sincere.

Consider the purpose of a compliment. Typically, it is to build rapport and make someone warm to you. You are being generous, observant and likeable. If they have pride in what you have commented on, chances are they will feel good about themselves and be more relaxed around you.

Let's face it, we live in rather selfish, self-serving and self-obsessed times. Society operates at a frantic and intense pace filled with negativity, trolls and criticism. A great way to make a mark with your colleagues, friends and family is to make them your focus, and build them up.

When it comes to you as a leader, ask yourself, what kind of leader are you? Do you help people see their strengths and potential? Or do you focus on yourself or the bottom line?

I read a study recently which stated that more than a third of people who leave their job do so because they feel underappreciated. Don't neglect the people around you . . . nurture them instead.

The key is getting the balance right. It is obvious when someone pays you a sincere compliment, and equally obvious when someone falsely tries to elevate you with an insincere compliment. This just feels patronising.

Another thing to be mindful of is when people have low self-esteem and your compliment doesn't match their own self-talk. Research conducted by the University of Leicester in the UK concluded that people tend to look for cognitive balance. When you flatter someone with high self-esteem, they will warm to you more because you are validating their own self-image. However, when you flatter someone with low self-esteem and it conflicts with their self-image, they may like you less or subconsciously question your judgement.

A Moment of Reflection

- What do you admire most about your best contacts, team, family, customers?
- Tell them!

Remember, for the accompanying strategy template and other resources go to www.InfluenceTheBook.com.

Express your values

'If you stay true to yourself and true to your vision and your own values, you can power through and make an impact on modern life.'

Stephen Bannon

One of the most satisfying things you can do in your personal and business life is to live your values. It is even better when we attract people to us who share these values with us.

For example, here are some of the values I hold dear.

- Integrity
- Positivity
- Creativity
- Developing people
- Transparency.

So, I like to work on projects or with people where these values are apparent. To attract such projects, I make sure I share my values when I speak on a stage, write a blog or simply in day-to-day conversations.

If, like me, you work for yourself, then it is easy to integrate your values into your brand. If you are working for someone else or a large brand, you can still infuse your values in your work and your daily interactions.

So, consider doing the following.

- Include your values in your company literature.
- Keep them front of mind on the walls of your place of work.
- Share them on your website.
- Share them on your business card.
- Include them in your stories.
- Compliment those who embody your values.

But perhaps more powerful than simply expressing your values is demonstrating them.

Many years ago, when my two children were very young, my wife and I decided to take them to Euro Disney in Paris on the Eurostar. We had a lot of fun – it was exhausting actually, which anyone with small kids will attest to. Anyway, we were on our homeward journey to London which is a three-hour train ride.

My wife settled into a good book and, on this occasion, I played children's entertainer with playing cards, games and colouring-in books (it was pre-iPad). What happens in this environment if you are relatively lively or fun, is that you start to attract the other children in the carriage.

Before long I was entertaining six kids while their parents looked on, grateful for the respite. It wasn't until the last 10 minutes of the journey, approaching London, that one of the fathers approached me and said thank you for generously including his child in the fun. He then asked the following question 'I'm intrigued, what you actually do for a living?'

This led to a conversation and an exchange of business cards. Three weeks later we had done business together. You see I had already won his trust; he could see my values in my actions. I was inclusive, generous with my time, caring, a family man etc. The relationship hadn't even started when he observed all of this so the rest was easy.

Are your actions congruent with your values? How could you integrate them more with your message?

If you haven't done so before, pause for a moment and write down what your values are. What is important to you? Then take a look at your website, your LinkedIn profile etc. Are they obvious?

A Moment of Reflection

- What are your business and personal values?
- If they aren't written down already, do so now.
- Take a look at your website, social profiles and marketing literature. How well do you think your values are reflected?
- What could you do to include them more?

Remember, for the accompanying strategy template and other resources go to www.InfluenceTheBook.com.

Manners Maketh Man

> *'One of the greatest victories you can gain over someone is to beat him at politeness.'*
>
> **Josh Billings**

There are many words to describe proper social behaviour – manners, politeness, etiquette, decorum, propriety, respectability, decency, civility, courtesy, rectitude – to name a few.

Confucius is often attributed with formulating the first rules of decorum and, ever since, the importance of etiquette has been questioned. For me there is no doubt that manners maketh man, in fact I have witnessed first-hand the advantages politeness can provide and the punishment for rudeness.

Many years ago, I attended my very first networking event. I was young, overconfident and ambitious, and walked into a room full of other business owners without fear (at least that is what I told myself).

Now, I had travelled to London for this event and didn't know a single person in the room. So I did the normal thing whilst I weighed up the situation and poured myself a coffee. A few metres away from me I recognised the name on someone's badge and thought to myself, there is my starting point.

His name was Reg and he was talking to someone else at the time, so I joined them. After about 20 minutes, Reg left the conversation and I turned to the other chap and asked his name and what he did. He told me his name was Will Kintish and he was a professional speaker.

'What do you speak on?' I asked.

'Networking' he replied.

With a cheeky smile on my face, I asked 'How am I doing?'

He paused, looked me in the eye, and with a very slight shake of his head said, 'You don't want to know.'

I, of course, with my overconfidence laughed and replied, 'No seriously, how am I doing?'

'You really don't want to know' came the reply.

A look of confusion came over my face and I remember feeling a little worried. There was a moment of awkwardness until I asked a third time. 'No really, I do want to know, please tell me.'

Will then proceeded to tell me all of the things I had done in that initial 20 minutes which had broken the etiquette of networking. Something I didn't even know existed by the way. He told me I had interrupted his conversation with Reg, proceeded to talk about myself, given Reg most of my attention and almost ignored Will . . . and about ten other things.

I was mortified. He then took me to the side of the room and with his back to the room proceeded to describe the body language and formations of people in the room; and it was at this point I realised there was so much more to this thing called networking.

More importantly, I was grateful that I received this baptism of fire on my very first event, rather than 20 years down the line when I probably would have developed more bad habits and been oblivious to the bad impression I was making.

You see, I didn't even know there was an etiquette. I will come back to Will Kintish later in this section, but if you are reading this Will: thank you.

So, how can manners help you influence others? I know people who think that manners hold less importance in today's fast-paced world, and that we don't have time for it. But I vehemently disagree.

How you treat others, both in the words you say and the actions you take, has a huge effect on how others perceive you. Politeness is to communication like warmth is to wax. It makes exchanges more cordial and transactions go smoother.

Have you ever been in a business meeting where someone in the room continually interrupts whoever is speaking before they have been allowed to finish their point? How did you feel about them?

Have you ever been ordered by a boss to do something rather than asked with a please? What impression did they make?

Now I know in some other cultures, particularly in the work environment, etiquette is given much less attention. But throughout the majority of the West it is a prized quality, worth developing.

If you use manners well, people will assume a good upbringing, strong morals and values, maybe a decent education. All good impressions to make.

A very dear friend of mine, Andrew Widgery, is the walking embodiment of a true English Gentlemen. I have learned bucketloads from him over the years and have been grateful for his friendship and mentorship.

Andrew is thoughtful, impeccably mannered, and utterly charming. He makes people feel good about themselves and treats others the way they want to be treated. As a result of this, people love to be around him, they feel empowered, validated and generally happier in themselves because of how he makes them feel.

Because of this, people go out of their way to be around him and do things for him. This is influence. This is something you can improve right now.

Learning or considering the etiquette of a situation before you dive in is probably the best advice I can give you in this section. For example, you wouldn't step on a golf course and insist on dispensing with etiquette, it would simply result in you being expelled from the course . . . eventually. In business, there is nothing to expel you from (well, maybe your job), but people will vote with their feet.

A friend of mine is a partner in a business and was seeking investment. He spent a lot of time courting several sophisticated, high net worth, potential investors and finally came to an agreement in principle, subject to due diligence.

One of the first requests was to go out to dinner with the rest of the management team, including his business partner, so they could meet the personalities involved in the business. Unfortunately, his partner was less refined and lacking in social skills, and at dinner proceeded to disgust the investors with expletives, coughing without covering his mouth and at one point instead of using the napkin to just wipe his mouth, used it to blow his nose.

Sure enough, the following day the investment was withdrawn. People like to do business with people they like.

So remember, in almost every situation there will be an etiquette, whether it's a meeting etiquette, workplace etiquette, table manners, conference call etiquette or cultural differences (if you work internationally). They are worthy of your attention.

Empathy and sincerity

> *'The biggest deficit that we have in our society and in the world right now is an empathy deficit. We are in great need of people being able to stand in somebody else's shoes and see the world through their eyes.'*
>
> **Barack Obama**

(And just for fun.)

> *'Before you criticize a man, walk a mile in his shoes. That way, when you do criticize him, you'll be a mile away and have his shoes.'*
>
> **Steve Martin**

The admonition to *walk a mile in someone else's shoes* simply means: before you judge anyone, you must understand their feelings, experiences, challenges, thought processes, conclusions etc. The complete idiom is: *Before you judge a man, walk a mile in his shoes.* Effectively this is a reminder to practise empathy.

Empathy can be simply described as the awareness of the emotions and feelings of other people. It is putting yourself in other people's shoes to understand what they are experiencing. Empathy is a key component of emotional intelligence and a powerful skill to use in all relationships.

It is not to be confused with sympathy, which is 'feeling for' someone as opposed to 'feeling with' someone through the use of imagination.

Have you ever said this about someone? 'That person just gets me' or 'we are on the same wavelength'? Whose name springs to mind? I bet you generally consider them 'good with people'. Well the chances are this person has genuine empathy. More importantly, they possess a key leadership quality which will enable them to influence.

Empathy is key to negotiation and, let's face it, life is negotiation.

Ambassador Dennis Ross, chief Middle East peace negotiator during the George H. W. Bush and Bill Clinton administrations, applied his empathy rule in all negotiations he was involved in. He said 'To gain the hardest concessions, prove you understand what is important to the other side . . . (and know) why certain concessions are so painful for it.'

I remember listening to a speech delivered by the ex-leader of the Conservative Party, William Hague (a very funny speaker by the way). In it he shared his story of the Northern Ireland peace process.

In the buildup to the final stages of the agreement, he had studied hard, understood the politics, had a deep technical understanding of the facts and history to date. Even on the short flight to Northern Ireland he was swotting up on the facts before he landed, while Tony Blair slept in the neighbouring seat. But when it came to getting the deal over the line, despite not being as knowledgeable, Tony Blair was amazingly empathetic, really tapping into the mood of the people.

So here are a few ideas for effectively using empathy in your day-to-day negotiations. More on negotiation to follow in the next section on diplomacy.

Ask Open-ended Questions

Empathy is almost impossible unless you understand the opposition viewpoint, so create the right atmosphere for gathering information and, of course, sharing your point of view.

Open-ended questions – using what, why, how, when and where, or phrases like 'explain to me', 'describe for me' etc. – are crucial because they send the message that you are truly interested. Whereas closed questions elicit one word answers, which ultimately can make people defensive.

Demonstrate Understanding

Simply saying you understand isn't enough. You can really demonstrate understanding through your body language and by relating to what you are being told, maybe sharing a similar experience you have had.

Use phrases to show you have really listened like 'I would feel exactly the same in your position' or 'Let me just make sure I fully appreciate what you are saying' then repeat it back to them.

Sincerity is critical

It's not good enough just asking questions if you are not really interested in the answers or your body language is incongruent with what you are saying.

If you just view empathy as a tool to manipulate, then the chances are it will be noticed, and it could do more harm than good. If you genuinely seek to understand others perspectives, then they will open up further and trust you.

Reciprocation and Concession

Don't for one minute think empathy is a one-way street. When used in negotiation, set the expectation that your perspective is also understood.

Fully appreciating the impact of concessions for both parties creates mutual understanding and compromise.

The art of diplomacy

> *'Diplomacy is the art of letting somebody else have your way.'*
>
> **David Frost**

Right at the beginning of the communication section I talked about intuition, which I believe plays a big role in diplomacy.

Tact and diplomacy are skills which are centred around understanding other people. This includes their opinions, ideology, ideas and of course the way they feel. Once you understand the way a person thinks you can respond in such a way as to avoid ill feeling or conflict, whilst simultaneously sharing your own ideas in a delicate well-meaning way.

Diplomacy is one of those life skills you wish everyone had. Sadly they don't. I am sure every one of us can name someone who is capable of talking their way out of most difficult situations, maybe sometimes it is luck, but more often than not they will naturally possess the skills listed below. Many of these key skills for being more diplomatic have already been discussed.

Listening. What is being said and what does it mean to them?

Communication Skills. Articulating your point of view clearly.

Self-Control. Controlling your temper, avoiding arguments and confrontation.

Confidence. Speaking with conviction.

Rapport. Getting on well with others.

Empathy. Putting yourself in someone else's shoes.

Good Manners. Observing etiquette and showing respect.

Emotional Intelligence. Understanding the emotions involved on both sides of the exchange.

Developing your diplomatic skills is a key part of negotiation which we touched on during the last section on empathy.

Whilst this isn't a book on negotiation, I believe it would be remiss of me, in a book focused on influence, not to touch on it. We all negotiate every day – whether it's a new contract, a pay rise, who's turn it is to get the coffee, a compromise at home or getting a child to do their homework.

Of course, a major part of negotiation is winning the trust of the other party. For them to trust you are seeking a win–win situation where you can both walk away satisfied with the outcome.

A great recent example of this was the Disney acquisition of LucasFilm in 2013, home of the tremendously well-known and successful *Star Wars* brand.

Disney were looking to cement their place further as the leader in the animation and superhero market following their earlier acquisitions of Pixar and Marvel; and a deal with LucasFilms would provide the opportunity for lucrative earnings from merchandising alone.

At the time, it was widely reported that George Lucas (the sole owner of LucasFilms) was tired of the pressure of living up to the expectations of the very opinionated *Star Wars* fans. In an interview, he said 'Why would I make any more [films] when every-body yells at you all the time and says what a terrible person you are?'

Lucas was also 68 years old and planning for his retirement, so for Disney CEO at the time, Robert A. Iger, the timing was probably right.

Despite this, the negotiation took over two years before the deal was done. Why was this? Well, Lucas was very wary of the approach at first. After all, *Star Wars* is his legacy, his defining work. Iger was mindful of this and conducted the negotiation himself, showing Lucas it was worthy of his personal attention.

Also, recognising how emotionally invested Lucas still was in his creation, he was offered a role in the new films they planned to release showing him they wanted to build on his vision rather than simply replace it.

Yes, it took time, but that's how long it took to build the trust. The deal finally settled at $4.05 billion – split evenly between stock and cash. Worth the wait for both parties considering Disney made over $2 billion alone from the worldwide box office from their first release and that doesn't include merchandising.

I thought it would be useful to share with you some ideas on how you can be more diplomatic in your negotiations.

Planning

Planning for a negotiation or difficult conversation is essential for understanding your desired outcome and preparing for the potential objections of the other party.

Write down your objectives and the reasons for them, and try to separate your personal feelings from the facts. Give consideration to what the objections might be from others and think carefully about how you might answer their objections. Preparing will show them you have given their concerns consideration.

Managing the Mood

This starts with you! Try not to enter a negotiation angry or stressed as this will affect your thinking and more likely make the other party more defensive.

Avoid negotiation fatigue syndrome. This is where your physical state (tiredness) can lead you to making compromises not in your best interests. Exploiting your tiredness is a strategy used and taught. Beware!

Try to keep an open mind at all times and stay calm. If you disagree with something, ask better questions and focus on the facts before you give a reaction. You can always ask for time to consider a point you passionately disagree with.

You can also manage the mood of the room. If you feel things are getting heated, request a break or instead practise the empathy techniques in the previous section.

Listen Empathetically

See the earlier section 'Empathy and sincerity'.

Negotiate

If your objectives are in conflict with those of the other person, then you may have to seek a compromise. Typically, sacrifices are made by both parties with the aim of creating a win–win situation.

Add Weight to Your Argument

There are several techniques for strengthening your position in a negotiation – from having the contract drawn up in advance to favouring facts and logic over personal feelings and being precise with the details (dates and numbers).

Turning your statements into questions will force the other party to think in a bit more detail rather than just react, and should allow for a more in-depth exploration of the possible outcomes.

Using immediacy can be powerful in the appropriate circumstances. A friend of mine buys second-hand cars and conducts the negotiation with the cash visibly in his hands. More often than not, people settle for what they can get right now rather than later.

Keep Your Eye on the Prize

Remember to keep your goals front of mind and try to stay focused. It's easy to get caught up in the details. Stay assertive, but not aggressive, and remember that being diplomatic does not mean caving in to others' demands.

Hopefully, these simple to implement strategies will give you a better advantage in all future negotiations.

Self-Deprecation

We love people who don't take themselves too seriously and can poke a little fun at themselves. It makes them seem humble and approachable. It can also be used to manage the expectations of our colleagues; for example, with a little self-deprecation you can avoid being put on a pedestal and ensure people don't expect too much. You may even win points for modesty.

As a speaker, I use self-deprecation a lot as it seems to make my audiences relax and become more receptive to new ideas. There is always that moment when a speaker walks on to a stage when you hope they are not patronising or full of themselves. As a result, we have our barriers up. Well some people do anyway. By making fun of myself and acknowledging the experience in the room early in my presentation, I find I can immediately create more rapport with my audience.

Now I wouldn't use self-deprecation everywhere. It can backfire in certain situations. For example, if you are in an interview situation you need to focus on your strengths. Whilst no one likes a boaster, you need to share your achievements in a way you are comfortable with and that is realistic.

Also, when someone pays you a compliment, if you're like me you might have a tendency to counterbalance it with a quip about an inadequacy. Whereas the only thing that should come out of your mouth is 'thank you'.

The real key to using self-deprecation is to know your audience. If you are very junior, then knocking yourself in front of your senior colleagues may not get you noticed for promotion. If, though, you are in a position of authority, self-deprecation will make you more approachable.

Ultimately, use it wisely but remember it can be very endearing, reminding us that we are all flawed human beings and that nobody is perfect.

A Moment of Reflection

- Reflect on your last few conversations, how well did you demonstrate the following?
  - o Manners
  - o Empathy
  - o Sincerity
  - o Your values.
- Reflect on your last few conversations, how well did you listen?
- When faced with conflict, how do you respond?

Remember, for the accompanying strategy template and other resources go to www.InfluenceTheBook.com.

WORDS THAT INFLUENCE

'Think twice before you speak, because your words and influence will plant the seed of either success or failure in the mind of others.'

Napoleon Hill

In the next section I will be taking a more in-depth look at demonstrating expertise, with writing playing a big part of that. But in the meantime, as part of communication, I want to take a look at some of the words that influence, both verbally and in written form.

I have talked about intonation previously – how the brain interprets meaning from what we say, how we say it and the facial expressions we use. Here I just want to focus on the words themselves, although there is some overlap between what we say and the way we say it.

The most influential people in the world understand how to use words and language intentionally; to inspire, motivate and win the hearts and minds of others.

But why is it that some words are more persuasive than others? Well, in recent years, there have been some fascinating studies which have challenged our previous conclusions.

Research conducted by Cambridge University and University College London using functional magnetic resonance imaging (fMRI) has revealed that a very specific part of the brain singles out speech near the primary auditory cortex. Which is amazing when you consider speech, like all other sounds, is just vibrating air-waves, yet it stands apart from other background noise.

But it gets better than this. It was also discovered that speech sepa-rates into words and melody, meaning the varying intonation we use to identify gender, mood and accent etc. is channelled over to the right side of the brain to a region more commonly stimulated by music, and the speech is channelled to the left temporal lobe to be processed.

As an aside, another really interesting part of the research showed that when we use homonyms (words with more than one meaning yet the same pronunciation and spelling), there is a flurry of activity in various parts of our brain while we decipher context (for exam-ple, the phrases 'the case was firm but fair' or 'the pupil of a kid').

I look forward to new findings from the fascinating work these universities do.

A quick point about writing: try to keep your sentences tight, espe-cially if it is marketing copy. A common mistake, often made by beginners, is to add fancy words into their narratives under the false illusion that these words will create better images. It was Mark Twain who said 'I didn't have time to write a short letter, so I wrote a long one instead.' And I think he is spot on.

I'm not saying less is always more, I'm just saying make each word relevant. It is common opinion amongst writers that too much unnecessary text will cause the reader to skip, especially in today's busy world. Using fewer words can build trust.

The same is true when selling. I was always taught, when you make the sale ... shut up! And, in a meeting, have you ever found yourself daydreaming when someone starts rambling or doesn't get to the point?

Back to words. It seems not all words were created equal. Before we examine some specific words that you might find useful, here are a few guiding principles.

Use the language of your audience

Common sense, I hope, but if people use Google to search for a 'motivational speaker', you wouldn't label your page 'motivational orator'.

I can think of one politician in recent times who won an election simply by using the language of his supporters.

Use precise words

Remember, using a thesaurus might seem like a good idea, but a synonym might just hold a slightly different meaning and confuse your audience, and a confused mind never buys!

> 'Using a thesaurus will not make you look smarter. It will only make you look like you are trying to look smarter.'
>
> **Adrienne Dowhan**

Use sensory words

The most influential words are sensory words, because they make your audience feel, hear, smell, taste or see what you are saying. You are more likely to evoke a response when you connect to people on an emotional level!

Use positive words

Research by Dr Andrew Newberg at Thomas Jefferson University and Mark Robert Waldman, a communications expert, concludes that when we allow negative words into our thoughts it triggers activity in our brain's fear centre (the amygdala), causing stress-producing hormones to flood our systems.

They write 'Angry words send alarm messages through the brain, and they partially shut down the logic-and-reasoning centers located in the frontal lobes.'

Whether negative words are written or spoken out loud, they affect both you and your listener/reader, increasing anxiety and irritability which will seriously diminish your potential to collaborate. This is why I avoid negative people.

People have dozens of cognitive biases, which are systematic errors in thinking that affect the decisions and judgements we make. Often they can control our lives in quite shocking ways.

When you understand some of these psychological insights, I believe you hold an advantage that is almost unfair. So before I say any more I urge you to be ethical in how you use any persuasion techniques. I have said it already, but people don't like to be manipulated, should they feel they are, it creates long-term damage.

Positive framing is just one of these cognitive biases, which concludes that people will react to a particular choice differently depending on how it is presented.

Two pioneers in this field were psychologists Daniel Kahneman and Amos Tversky whose vast work has contributed hugely to our understanding of human behaviour. One experiment they conducted presented treatment options, for a hypothetical deadly disease affecting 600 people, in two different ways: positively and negatively.

The scenario presented positively asked participants to choose between Treatment A where 200 lives would be saved and Treatment B where there was a 33% chance that all would be saved but a 66% chance that no one would be saved.

Treatment A was chosen by 72% of participants.

Then the same treatments were presented negatively: Treatment A will result in 400 people dying and with Treatment B there is a 33% chance that no one will die and a 66% probability that all 600 will die.

This time only 22% chose Treatment A.

Even though the outcomes were identical, the results were enlightening as to the way we make decisions.

Now the marketers amongst you might be thinking 'yes well fear of loss is also a powerful cognitive bias and doesn't this conflict?'

There is no conflict and both are powerful allies when making your persuasive arguments, presenting to prospects, speaking from the stage or motivating an outcome.

You can maximise your message by expressing risk in negative terms but presenting your solution positively.

Positive communication is one of the most powerful ways to improve your relationships. It is attractive, contagious and makes a conversation flow better. When using positive language with the right tone and body language (as previously discussed) you have a winning formula.

So, let us look at some specific words.

What's in a name?

> 'A person's name is to that person, the sweetest, most important sound in any language.'
>
> **Dale Carnegie**

How many of you remember the story of Rumpelstiltskin? For those who don't, he was the central character in a Brothers Grimm fairytale published in 1812.

Rumpelstiltskin was an imp-like magical creature who you held power over if you knew his name. I believe our names have a certain power over all of us and can be used to build rapport very simply.

Our name is our identity, used to get our attention right from day one: remember the call from your mum or teacher? Our brain registers when our name is used and we instinctively turn towards the speaker, we have been conditioned to do this from birth. Even in a noisy room, someone saying our name cuts through the noise and gets noticed.

Think for a second about your own experience. Don't you instinctively want to get on with people who share your name? One of my favourite entrepreneurs is Warren Buffett, but I can't honestly say he would be if he were known by another name.

Using someone's name when you meet them lets them know they were worthy of remembering, they will feel respected and more important, and it is an essential step to making a connection. Every time you use their name in conversation you pull their attention back to what you are saying.

Charismatic people use names to great effect. They make every person they talk to feel like the most important person in the room. Your name will be the first thing they ask for and will probably be the last thing they say to you when they leave.

They will look you in the eyes when they use it and they will include it in questions like 'So David, what brings you to this event?' or 'Do you live locally Sarah?' Every time they use it you feel important, your ego massaged, like they are listening to you and you alone.

Twenty years ago, I had a lodger who worked for Virgin. He wasn't in a senior position in the organisation, just a young man in the early stages of his career. He told me of the time he attended his work Christmas party which was held at Richard Branson's estate.

As he entered the room he was greeted by Richard Branson himself, and more importantly, by his first name. He said 'Welcome Guy, I am really glad you could make it'. Apparently, he greeted every single member of staff that evening by their first name as they entered. A class act indeed, I suspect every one of them felt special in that moment.

Now I don't expect he had remembered everyone's name, I am sure he had someone whisper in his ear as they approached. But he still took the time to make his people feel special because he understands the power of a name.

A very good friend of mine, Rob Brown, who is also a Capstone author by the way, is probably the best I have seen at using this trick. We meet as part of the same mastermind group six times a year, usually in a nice country hotel. As soon as he arrives he learns the names of the hotel staff, and uses them naturally in all interactions. The service he receives is always second to none and the relationship he has with them is that little bit more personal.

So, think back to a time when you didn't remember someone's name. You probably felt awkward or avoided having to address them. Or have you ever got someone's name wrong? Did you feel embarrassed? How do you think it made them feel?

I have heard many excuses for why people can't remember a name . . . poor memory, not paying attention, age etc. They may even be true, but you can improve and here are a few ideas to help you.

Repeat it back to them   When someone first shares their name with you, say it back to them with a 'hello [Insert name]' or 'pleased to meet you [Insert name]'. It helps with early rapport and hopefully imprints it in your mind.

Repeat it in your head Take a close look at their features and characteristics whilst repeating their name in your head. This will anchor the word to the appearance.

Think of their namesake This is one I use. Picture them standing beside a famous namesake.

The associative method Convert the name to the nearest sounding word or words that pop into your mind. For example, Ben = Big Ben, Helen = Entrance to Hell, Mike = Microphone. Actually picture the image to match the words.

Ask for pronunciation OK, if their name is Bob then this might seem strange, but great for unusual names and shows them you care about getting their name right.

Don't overdo it! If you use it too much, it may come across as manipulation, which is likely to irritate or make them more guarded. For example, 'Hi Dave, I want to share with you Dave something interesting. Dave, do you have a few moments Dave?' LOL I am sure you wouldn't.

It's all about *you*

It may be second best to using a person's name, but *you* is right up there as one of the most powerful words in marketing for a good reason. It's personal to you, and it acts as a placeholder for your name.

Unlike your name, which if overused can sound a little creepy, the word 'you' is natural to use without the fear of overuse, yet still strokes our egos like our name does.

Let's talk about you for a minute. You is your most interesting subject; let's be honest, when the conversation is on you, I have your full attention. If I talk about an idea to make people success-ful, you may be interested, but if I talk about an idea to make you rich, you are all ears!

I see too many websites where the copy is 'weeing' all over the page. If you can do one thing for yourself this year which will make a difference, change all your 'we' phrasing to 'you' phrasing on your websites, social profiles and marketing messages.

'You' phrasing forces you to think how your reader/listener thinks, and it is this deeper understanding of their needs which you need to have in order to take the conversation further.

Imagine

Imagine if you had the power to influence people's subconscious minds by the words you say and the words you write. Imagine if you could engage people on an emotional level, building deeper more meaningful relationships. Now, whatever you do don't imag-ine a pink elephant dancing in top of a London taxi cab.

I bet you did it. ;-)

If you were to ask someone you had only just met for the first time to do something for you, chances are you would meet some resist-ance. It is natural for our critical minds to question instructions, particularly from a stranger.

However, this doesn't happen if you simply ask them to imagine an outcome. This is because the word imagine is one of the few words in the English language that has zero resistance to it because we don't see it as a 'real' task, just make believe.

By asking someone to imagine something you effectively enter their mind through the back door, and the brain cannot differentiate between its imagined reality and its experienced reality. As far as your brain is concerned, it can't tell the difference between imagining the ocean and seeing the ocean.

So, by helping people imagine your mutually beneficial outcome, it is far more likely they will accept it as reality.

There is a reason number one and number two in the smartphone marketplace have used the slogans 'Imagine' (Samsung) and 'Think Different' (Apple).

Because

> 'Because you're worth it.'
>
> ### L'Oreal

Another famous slogan, this time used by the cosmetic giant L'Oreal, utilises another powerful word: because.

'Because' is effective in persuasion because it's another word that bypasses our critical thinking to directly stimulate the unconscious mind. You see, as humans, we need reasons and explanations. We crave order, especially when it relates to us directly.

When our critical minds hear the word 'because', they assume a valid reason will follow and are more receptive. I have heard it said that this relates back to our childhood. As children we are naturally inquisitive about the world around us, always asking the question 'why?' to which our parents reply 'because' (hopefully followed by an explanation).

Even if there is no valid explanation, it can be used as a command:

'Mum, can I have some chocolate?'
'No'
'Why not?'
'Because I said so!'

We were taught that whatever followed 'because' was the valid reason or explanation. This is often referred to as the reason-why reflex.

I am reminded of a story from Dr Kevin Hogan when he worked with a charity on one of their marketing campaigns. Changing the end of their advert from 'Donate now' to 'Donate now, because it's really important' saw a 28% increase in donations.

So remember this when asking for a raise, or asking a colleague for help. Adding a reason will increase your chance of compliance, and the better the reason, the stronger your chance.

'Now', 'quickly', 'immediately', 'fast' and 'instantly': time-critical words

Humans are hardwired to want stuff . . . NOW. It's called instant gratification and, if used appropriately, it can help you create incredible appeal in your communications.

In most psychological models people are believed to act upon the pleasure principle, the driving force that compels us to gratify our urges, wants and needs. These can be as basic as food and water or as sophisticated as the latest iPhone.

Failing to get instant gratification leaves us unfulfilled, tense and anxious.

Several MRI studies have shown that our mid-brain gets fired up when we envisage instant gratification, and how our frontal cortex is activated instead if we have to wait. This is a disadvantage for the sales process as the frontal cortex is particularly active when we control impulsive behaviour.

Words like 'fast', 'instant', 'now' and 'immediately' can be triggers for firing up that mid-brain activity to take action.

One of my closest friends is a bed retailer and their advertising slogan is 'Order by lunchtime, delivered by bedtime'. Like all good advertising, this headline highlights a benefit and promises urgency.

'Now' is also one of those embedded commands from childhood. Remember when our parents asked us to go to bed, and we asked for just 15 more minutes, only to receive the command 'NOW'. There was no negotiation after 'now'.

Please and thank you

What's the magic word? I hope you didn't say 'abracadabra'.

Do you see the theme here of influential words which our parents taught us to be influenced by? We were taught to use 'please' and 'thank you' when we wanted something but we were equally taught to comply when they were used on us.

I'm not going to labour the point on this one because it is obvious and we have already covered manners and etiquette, but I cannot stress enough how important it is, especially today, to use the magic word.

Another thing to consider when you use 'please' is that you are typically asking for something. Studies show that, when it comes to our happiness, providing support is just as important to us as receiving support. By giving people the opportunity to help you, you generate good feelings in them and increase trust.

Many people don't like asking for help, but consider this: doing a favour, or asking for a favour, usually ends up strengthening relationships. Especially when appreciation is sincerely shown.

'In charge', 'ownership', 'risk free', 'guarantee' and 'no obligation': control words

Control words give us a sense of security and create the perception that things are in 'our control' and therefore it is safe to continue.

People love to believe that they control any given situation, including the sales cycle. If you can give them some peace of mind from the beginning, they will be more likely to have confidence to complete the process.

The word 'guarantee' is present in most good marketing copy, providing prospects with a safety net should things go wrong, but also confidence that they will be happy with their decision.

Studies in behavioural science have shown that people intrinsically fear loss. The fear of loss is a very powerful incentive for action. Whether that is losing money, respect, an opportunity or the loss of one's self-esteem, anything we can do to allay those fears with a guarantee or the feeling of control will smooth any transaction.

The fear of loss can also be used to remind someone of what they stand to lose should they not proceed with a particular course of action. As long as our fear-based arguments are true and ethical, of course.

'Free'

Everybody loves 'free'. Like the control words above, free implies 'no risk'.

'Free' taps into our aversion to loss, we simply hate missing out on things and will naturally pursue low hanging fruit.

However, a word of caution when using 'free'. We have built a little resistance to it and some will treat with scepticism. You have heard the phrase 'If something is too good to be true it usually is', right? Think about it, when was the last time you saw 'free' and it really meant free? Or did it ask you to fill out a direct debit mandate followed by pages of small print?

Also, having free things may attract more people, but you will get your fair share of bargain hunters who may not in the long run be your ideal customers.

I remember speaking with a garage several years ago who promoted a deal on Groupon for people to have their MOT done at a bargain price (for non-UK readers an MOT is a compulsory, annual safety test for your car). Their hope was that, if there was work to be carried out, they would pick up that too making the bargain a loss leader. Well, the thing about the bargain hunter mentality is that they took advantage of the offer, but then went elsewhere to get all corrective work done on the cheap. It ended up costing the garage money and was their first and last Groupon experiment.

'New'

The word 'new' is often considered paradoxical because whilst humans are typically resistant to change, we also like the novelty of new things. In fact, every time we receive new things the reward centre in our brain is activated. Remember how you feel when you receive your new smartphone and remove the packaging?

'New' is particularly effective when used with products because customers appreciate new features, a fresh new design and new innovations. Be careful with services, though, as you don't want to appear a 'Jack of all trades, master of none': favour instead a 'fresh approach', a 'new way of thinking', and so on.

'Aware', 'realise' and 'experience'

These are three of my favourite words to use, especially when speaking, because they cause your audience to mentally process the point you are making and it is generally accepted that every-thing that follows is presupposed to be true.

'You may have already experienced how easily you can . . . '
'You are probably already aware of the fact . . . '
'I am sure you realise by now . . . '

As with all of the word examples I have used in this chapter, the secret to mastering language is to test and play with it. If written copy, test and compare different styles. If verbal, watch reactions to see if your point has more impact, or ask for feedback.

A Moment of Reflection

- Having read this chapter, how would you rate your website and marketing copy?
- Take some time to rephrase your key messages using the words that influence.

Remember, for the accompanying strategy template and other resources go to www.InfluenceTheBook.com.

5
K IS FOR KNOWLEDGE

It is not enough to know stuff; people need to know you know stuff! I make no apologies, this is going to be a really meaty section of the book.

DEMONSTRATING EXPERTISE

I am often asked how one should go about demonstrating expertise, particularly by people at the beginning of their journey who have no proof, no case studies or customer testimonials and no clients yet. I have friends who have spent decades applying expertise on behalf of their employers where the recognition goes to the company and not them. When they decide to go it alone they definitely have expertise, but they are almost anonymous to search engines, their target audience and their industry peers. Here is what I tell them.

Actually, before I answer 'how', let's explore 'why', in the context of influence, it is important to share what you know.

Essentially, almost all business decisions are based on confidence, and I believe the most effective way to establish confidence is to demonstrate your expertise.

Behavioural economics examines how we make financial decisions, and you might be surprised by the reality. Many would assume we make rational decisions that are in our best interests, right? Actually, no. Most people when faced with important decisions procrastinate due to feeling unsure and confused. This is when they are most likely to turn to a trusted advisor, especially one they have been recommended or who has given them confidence through a display of their knowledge.

As a sales tool this can be very powerful; for example, have you ever seen a law firm offer a free initial consultation? Why would they do this? Well it serves three purposes.

First the prospect will feel less pressure and therefore will arrive feeling relaxed, because they know they have no obligation to buy. **Second**, as discussed in a previous chapter, should they realise as a result of the consultation that they do indeed need to proceed with a lawyer, they will feel a deep desire to reciprocate because they have received valuable advice for free. **Third**, a free consultation is a perfect chance to gain the prospect's confidence by showing them you know what you are talking about. By taking the time to understand their issues and provide clarity on the next steps you have already started to earn their trust.

It really does surprise me that many other industries don't use the term 'free consultation' as opposed to free quote. Anyone providing a service can become the trusted advisor by adding value and providing clarity first.

It is my firmly held opinion that anyone who has been part of a workforce for a period of time will have at least some level of professional expertise. Your unique experiences, skills and knowledge make you an asset, and in order to create influence this needs to be shared.

I have met many people over the years who consider knowledge as power and as a result they keep it to themselves, only giving snippets when they have to. This is a form of self-preservation and comes from their own need to feel important. Essentially, they are insecure.

But I believe knowledge is a gift that deserves to be shared with others, and there are many benefits to doing so.

Sharing your knowledge enriches and expands what you know. In fact, it is probably the most effective way to deepen your knowledge further, as you will hone your message, find more effective ways to communicate it and, when recipients of your knowledge seek clarity or challenge your thinking, the chances are you will learn something new providing you keep an open mind.

During the process of writing this book, my knowledge has deepened through my research and through the challenges from my proofreaders and editor. Every time I deliver a speech my knowledge deepens as I need to be constantly aware of all the latest developments within my field, therefore I keep my knowledge up to date but I also learn from the audience's challenging questions. Learn to embrace these challenges. Even if you know them to be wrong, you are learning about other people's perceptions and maybe how best to change them.

> *'Knowledge is like money: to be of value it must circulate, and in circulating it can increase in quantity and, hopefully, in value.'*
>
> **Louis L'Amour**

Sharing your knowledge increases your value. Whether it is your team, your clients or your prospects, by giving freely you become more valuable by helping them raise their level of expertise and strengthening your relationship. Better still, you create advocacy and quickly establish your reputation as an authority and a leader in your field . . . you become the '**go-to person**'.

Most of the great connectors I know have done this. They are valuable to their networks because they give freely to them. I have many 'go-to people' for different industries, professions, geographical locations etc. Their names instantly spring to mind if a relevant challenge arises and they have the right contacts and authority to help me tackle it. As a result they are always in the mix when new opportunities come about.

For people with limited marketing budgets, sharing knowledge can also be a cost-effective way to raise awareness and attract publicity.

So, now that we have made the case for demonstrating expertise, let's look at ways in which we can do it.

For me the answer rests in 4 P's – Publish, Public Speaking, Publicity and Profile – and they are as relevant for established leaders as they are for those at the beginning of their journey.

LET'S START WITH PUBLISHING

Publishing can take many forms, sharing knowledge on social media, writing articles on LinkedIn, commenting on other people's content, blogging, writing for a magazine or writing a book are all forms of publishing and can all help elevate your status.

We are continually surprised by the speed that online publishing and social media can influence buying decisions and build trust. But don't forget there are still opportunities in print publishing worth including in your strategy.

Even the most experienced marketers are still learning every day about what works and what doesn't; and the beautiful thing about writing across multiple platforms is you can repurpose your content for use in different places.

Over the next few chapters we will take a look at the various publishing options open to you, the pros and cons and strategies to get started.

Blogging

So, let us start by talking about blogging. Whilst the origins of blogging were people sharing personal online journals in a 'we**b log**', it has evolved significantly since. In fact, typical of most internet innovations, entrepreneurs quickly spotted the opportunity to use blogs for marketing purposes and even financial gain, i.e. a business in its own right.

There is still much confusion about what constitutes a blog over a website, and this is in part because many companies have both and often integrate them using a single domain. But there are in fact two features of a blog which differentiate it from a website: 1. blogs are regularly updated with new content added several times a week, and 2. blogs encourage engagement with your audience, making them social.

Creating your own blog and posting regularly is an easy, low cost way to start sharing your knowledge ...

So, before I tell you how to get started, let me share why you should in the first place (and I apologise in advance for the stat attack). Even if you don't consider yourself a writer, I encourage you to blog. Here's why.

Businesses that Use Blogs Get More Leads and Ultimately More Sales

According to InsideView, B2B marketers that use blogs create 67% more leads than those that don't; and according to HubSpot, 92% of companies who blog regularly say they win customers from their blog.

This isn't surprising when you consider that a blog helps you create a bigger presence on the internet both with links to your website (companies that blog have 97% more inbound links) and more indexed pages (companies that blog receive 434% more indexed pages on average), because search engines love new content. As a result, blogging is a great search engine optimisation (SEO) tool.

I find it astounding that only 33% of brands actually blog ... Why is this, given the results?

It's not rocket science, more traffic = more leads = more sales! But let's not stop there. After all, we are talking about building influence and trust.

Blogging Will Help You Build Trust with Your Audience

So, in terms of consumer confidence, research shows that 9 out of 10 consumers have made purchases after reading about a product or service on a blog. In fact, it's considered more influential than Facebook, YouTube and LinkedIn. So why is this?

Well, in a blog you can show off what you know, which will build your expertise and credibility. Also, on a blog you tend to find a more honest and sincere review of a product or service where the negatives are highlighted as well as the positives, this in turn creates more trust in the author as someone impartial and transparent. Ultimately though, trust drives action!

As I have said before, we live in an age of due diligence, where people do their homework before making decisions. Again, according to HubSpot, 79% of online shoppers spend over 50% of shopping time researching!

Engagement with your audience warms them to you and helps you establish authority with them. Someone is far more likely to take your call if they have already read your thought leadership.

It really is a great way to keep your customers and clients up to date, provide tips and advice and even offer new deals. The more someone visits, the more likely they will spend.

According to a report on Digital Influence by Technorati, 86% of influencers blog, and 88% of those do so for themselves rather than their brand. There is only one conclusion to draw from this, if YOU do in fact want to be more influential.

Blogging Will Help You Grow Your Audience

We live in a time when someone who will never ever buy from you can still contribute to your bottom line by simply liking and sharing your content with someone who will buy. SO MAKE IT EASY FOR THEM TO SHARE!

There are many simple strategies to drive more traffic, whether it is through your marketing literature, email or social media. Or search engines because you have optimised your content, used the right keywords or written about the things people search for. Or, lastly, other people who share your stuff because it was simply worthy of sharing – you know, helpful, inspiring, provocative, controversial, topical and so on.

For more ideas around driving traffic, see my website Influence TheBook.com *and join the conversation.*

Blogging Makes You a Better Thought Leader

The simple process of writing helps you to order your thoughts and allows you to think deeper on your topic. You will undoubtedly research more and show interest in what your peers have to say.

Writing a blog means you can constantly add your expertise to the industry discussion and potentially even turn your blog into a knowledge centre. Encourage the conversation from your audience by allowing user comments which, in turn, will help guide and inspire future content. As mentioned previously, comments will also challenge your thinking, forcing you to come up with more robust arguments.

It won't be long before you are recognised as an expert in your field, but please don't make the mistake so many people do and start selling. Remember, it is about providing value and building trust.

Blogging Makes You a Better Communicator

As with all forms of communication, the more you do it the better you become. The simple act of writing your opinions down, in order to be persuasive so your readers will agree with you, will help you find new ways to articulate your argument. This in turn impacts the way you speak on your subject, giving you more clarity and impact.

For me, writing has made me more rational, more logical and has helped me to order my thoughts. This has impacted my communication way beyond my work and helped me relate better to my children and wider social relationships.

Blogging Will Make You a Better Opportunist

Your quest for new content ideas will mean that you are always receptive, looking for an angle. Every day things will inspire you and keep your subject front of mind.

Here is a quote I love:

> 'Opportunity dances with those already on the dancefloor.'
>
> **H. Jackson Brown Jnr.**

To me, this translates into 'you are more likely to find something if you are already looking for it'. You are more likely to notice stuff relating to your business, area of expertise, if it is always front of mind.

Let me give you an example. Have you ever bought a new car, and in the weeks that follow you suddenly spot the same model, make – even colour – all over the place? They were always there. It is just now they are front of mind and therefore easier to spot.

This works beyond writing of course. Remind yourself daily of the things you want, and you are much more likely to spot the opportunities that relate to them. It's obvious if you think about it.

Lastly, blogs make money. As well as your product or service, you can monetise a blog by selling advertising, sponsorship and affiliate revenue.

Which platform?

So, now we have explored why you should blog, let's look at how you get started.

Choosing a platform is the first decision you need to make. There are many free options out there (WordPress, Tumblr, Blogger and TypePad) which all offer free design themes so you can customise look and feel.

I personally recommend self-hosting a WordPress site for the simple reasons that your traffic is your own, you can commercialise your content much easier and you have more flexibility around design and functionality. There is a ton of useful content online helping you get set up so I won't repeat that here.

Find your niche

The cost of a domain is minimal and, if you have a business website already, you are probably better served driving more traffic to that than you are sending your readers elsewhere. I recommend picking a domain name that is functional and relates to your content for the search engine benefit. Remember, you want to be easily found for your topic.

Wherever possible, try and niche down your content. By making your blog about something very specific you will get more benefit from search engines and really please your readers. When people are too general they rarely get known for specific areas of expertise, remember you want your name to spring to mind every time your topic comes up.

So, to find your niche you really need to identify your audience and take time to understand their needs. OK, I know where they are, how do I get them to read?

Build your ability to drive traffic

Once you have identified your audience and decided on your niche, it should be much easier to drive relevant traffic. You can write brilliant content or produce excellent videos, but if no one is watching then what is the point?

You won't get anywhere with the mantra 'If you build it, they will come'; yes, it worked for Kevin Costner in *Field of Dreams*, but in my experience hope is not a strategy.

You really need to have a focus on marketing, and there are a number of ways successful bloggers do this from guest posting, to commenting on others' posts, to building an influential social media presence.

Where does your audience play on social media? Join those groups, follow, connect and build relationships. Start to build your list and communicate with it regularly; consider a newsletter. Remember you want to be front of mind with them, and regular contact will help you achieve that.

Once identified, what attracts them?

Give value to your readers

Don't just think of your blog as an opportunity to sell stuff. Add value to your readers and they are more likely to share your content and return to your site for the next instalment.

Invite ideas for content from your audience, solve their problems, answer their questions, explain away their confusion and you will soon attract fans. The more you understand your readers, the easier it is to create content that resonates with them.

A simple technique to test what content your readers are interested in is to test with social media. I know several bloggers who tweet quotes or questions just to see what response they get. A good response is an obvious subject for a more in-depth post.

Another way to add value and build your list is to give things away: how-to guides, tutorials, checklists and so on.

Your blog is your ability to showcase what you know. Be generous with your knowledge and you will reap the rewards.

What attracts readers in the first place?

Great Headlines

There are several aspects to attracting readers. It all starts with the headline. We live in an age where attention spans are shrinking, so you only have a split second to convince a potential reader to click, and it is your headline that will draw them in. As a rule, keep them simple, compelling, useful and bold.

Consider using lists '10 Reasons to . . . ', '12 Tips for . . . ', '8 Epic Fails . . .' for example; or education-focused content, e.g. 'A Beginners Guide to . . .', 'An Introduction to . . .' all of which, according to research, draws in a reader and inspires their curiosity. People want to learn, so teach them.

A Picture is Worth a Thousand Words

Yes, I know this is a massive cliché, but it is true and supported by science. Time to geek out a little . . .

Consider the fact that our oldest evidence of pictorial communication as a species dates back to around 30,000BC with cave drawings, yet the earliest evidence of writing dates back to late 4000BC. So, this means that thoughout the vast majority of our history we have had to communicate without the written word, and it is therefore easy to conclude that we are hardwired for visual data.

The speed at which our brains translate visual data verses text based data is significant also. It is, in fact, 60,000 times faster. A whopping 40% of nerve fibres to the brain are connected to the retina. Of all information sent to the brain, 90% is visual – and 93% of all human communication is visual too.

Everything from body language (detailed in Chapter 4, Communication), road signs, advertising, facial expressions, to maps and gestures are forms of visual communication we see every day. So, it is not difficult to understand why we have adapted to discern visual concepts more efficiently.

It is our attraction to images which has given rise to mobile apps like Instagram, Pinterest, Snapchat and Vine and this is a trend which continues to influence the ongoing evolution of Facebook too.

According to the National Center for Biotechnology Information, the average customer's attention span has fallen from 12 seconds to 8 seconds since the year 2000. A 30% reduction in attention and officially one second less than a bloody goldfish!

Simply put, our capacity to focus is reducing, making it even more imperative to make an impact with the initial impression.

Retailers and big companies understand why this is important, building brands which are instantly, visually recognisable. Using the 8-second rule, it takes the human brain less than a second to process a single image or brand logo, leaving them 7 seconds to engage with a message or call to action.

So geek out over what that means for your blog!

Simply put, a strong image to accompany your post is more likely to attract a reader, especially when alongside a compelling headline. Research shows that a page with an image or video will attract on average 94% more views.

> Be sure to use images you have the rights to use. Many people fall foul of fines for using other people's images.

Video Blogging

So, it naturally, visually, follows to start video blogging also, preferably hosting your video on the second biggest search engine on the planet . . . YouTube.

If you are someone who can become comfortable on camera, then you have an advantage over your competition. Landing pages with video convert customers 86% more frequently than those with just text and motionless images.

All of the same content you would ordinarily write about, you can speak about. Just look at the fact that over a billion videos are played every day on Facebook – and over 65% of these are on a mobile device – and realise your blogging traffic is no longer relying on someone being sat at a desk, your audience can access your thought leadership from anywhere . . . and they will.

Tell Stories

I discussed story telling in Chapter 4. Stories in your blog will draw people in, build suspense, fire the imagination, create a deeper connection to the content and keep them wanting more.

Authenticity

This is a subject I will go into in a lot more detail in the next chapter, but in the context of blogging I implore you to be true to your voice. In my experience, when people deviate from their authentic voice they lose readers because it shows.

Don't be afraid to be personal (if appropriate for your profession/brand). A little vulnerability goes a long way, as does self-deprecating humour. The more you reveal about who you are, the more people will buy into you!

Add your picture to the posts you write with a one paragraph 'about' section. People want to follow people, not brands.

Be Easy to Read: Properly Format and Proofread your Work

Research suggests that people scan web pages rather than focus on every last bit of copy. So, try to keep your blogs as quick, easy reads and break up your content with line breaks, images, sub-heads, bullets, captions and so on. Short sentences win!

Your mission is to convert the scanner into a reader. This means getting them engaged.

Also, avoid clutter. When designing your site, try to keep a clean layout with plenty of white space. Keep it easy on the eye, avoiding unnecessary features.

Get the balance right with your word count. As a rule, try to write more than 300 words (which is better for search engines and attention spans) and no more than 1200. Obviously, there will be occasions when your content is by necessity much longer, but you can still make this easier to read or maybe consider turning it into several posts.

Lastly, keep an eye on the formatting, spelling and grammar. Whilst the majority of millennials probably won't care too much, I know plenty of pedants who would find poor punctuation a distraction – even worse, a frustration – and therefore a reason not to return. More importantly, it will have an adverse effect on your credibility as people will think you don't care enough to get it right.

Be Easy to Share – Get Social!

The best way to get people to share your content is to make it worth referencing, better still make it epic and original. We live in a busy, distracted world where you have to earn attention. Have a point and don't just vomit words on a page. Be bold in your writing and have an opinion, there is nothing wrong with writing with conviction.

Try and make sure each blog has an actionable item or an original idea/lesson. Try to think before you write what will make this worthy of sharing. Ask yourself the simple question 'Would anyone want to email this to a friend?' Don't publish until you think the answer is yes.

Next, make it easy to share. There is no excuse for not socialising your content so others can conveniently tweet or share. Don't be afraid to ask your readers to share either . . . finishing a piece with 'I hope you found value in this blog, if you did please share and help spread the word' is not going to offend anyone.

While you are at it, use social channels yourself to connect with new readers and other bloggers. Promote your content through your social channels and have strategies to build your sphere of influence.

As well as asking for the share, ask for the follow . . . and follow back! The ideal scenario is a future two-way conversation with your audience . . . so encourage it.

Lastly, the best way to create community and keep people coming back is to make commenting easy. Content that is interactive is sticky. Being able to exchange ideas with the author is attractive. Remember what I said earlier, they will challenge you and deepen your knowledge, this will inspire new content and you will develop more trusted relationships. What's not to like?

Some General Advice

Consistency is key   It is much easier to lose your traffic than it is to build it in the first place. According to Hubspot, blogs that publish more than once a week add more subscribers (more than twice as quickly) than those that publish once a month.

Remember it's not a short-term strategy   The internet is a big noisy place with millions of sites competing for the same eyeballs. Very rarely is there a short-term return on investment. But fortune favours the brave bloggers who are prepared to endure, refine, learn and hone their message.
That said, it is not all just about traffic. Remember, we live in an age of due diligence and the people you meet face to face will be checking you out and be reassured by you demonstrating your expertise online.

Don't forget a call to action   As mentioned above, but worth repeating. Don't rely on your readers taking action. Plant the seed firmly in their heads with a call to action, whether it be to share, follow you, like, click a link to a related post, download an amazing giveaway etc. Remember: Passive Posting Produces Piss Poor Performance!

Google proof your content   Or in other words, research properly, avoid speculation and stick to the facts. Of course, if you are writing an opinion piece then that's different, but support your opinions with research, they will be far more credible.

Write timeless content   Old content on the web is perceived to be irrelevant, so avoid writing about current events as if they had just happened. Remember, you are trying to build a resource, not a newspaper, so this might be a reason to remove dates from your posts. The flipside of this is search engines like established content, so in many cases older articles will achieve better search results.

Guest post regularly   Using the influence principle 'credibility by association', why not invite prominent thinkers in your field to write a guest article for you? This has many benefits from driving new traffic (especially if they promote their piece to their followers), to showing you rub shoulders with other influencers, thus raising your credibility. If they don't want to write a post, ask if you can interview them.

Wherever possible, and whenever invited, write back for them. They probably have more traffic than you, so send them your very best work.

In fact, as a strategy, guest posting is one of the most powerful ways for you to find new audiences, and I urge you to actively seek out opportunities to collaborate with other bloggers. Think about it, each one of them is an influencer in their own right, and allowing you to blog on their sites is effectively an endorsement.

And lastly . . . to quote Taylor Swift:

Haters gonna hate   Don't worry about negativity. Occasionally you may receive a negative comment on your blog but this is rare. I actually believe a few haters is usually a sign you are doing something right. Don't let it scare you off. Remember . . .

> *'No one ever achieved greatness by playing it safe.'*
>
> **Harry Gray**

A Moment of Reflection

- Whether you already blog or intend to start, consider the answers to the following questions.
  - What is the main subject and how does it help you?
  - Who is the intended audience?
  - What do you want them to do as a result of your writing?
  - Where does your audience hang out on social media?
  - Who is already successfully blogging that you can model?
  - Who could you invite to guest post?
  - What sites would you like to guest post for?

Remember, for the accompanying strategy template and other resources go to www.InfluenceTheBook.com.

Thought Leadership Websites

> 'True intuitive expertise is learned from prolonged experience with good feedback on mistakes.'
>
> **Daniel Kahneman**

There are several social platforms specifically designed to share expert opinion. LinkedIn to a certain extent does this, as does Quora. A key part of your strategy for demonstrating expertise should be to contribute content and engage with other people's content on these sites.

Ultimately, we want to raise your profile as a thought leader and show off your expertise. Actively participating in the conversations relating to your industry is one of the best ways to demonstrate your authority in your field. By sharing good advice and answering questions (not salesy), you will establish yourself as a go-to resource.

Groups on LinkedIn are a good place to start, just searching groups for keywords relating to your industry will reveal several I am sure. Don't just lurk on the sidelines, get involved.

Quora is more about following topics than following people. During 2016, their traffic averaged over 300 million visitors a month.

People ask questions on a variety of different topics which are open for anyone to answer, which is an ideal environment to demonstrate expertise. Participation is key.

A benefit of answering people's questions is that you won't come across as pushy or salesy, more like helpful. You will be doing nothing more than simply sharing ideas and expertise with an audience that is already engaged on the topic.

You can customise your profile for each topic that you follow or you can use the same one for all topics, which is clever.

So, with authority sites my simple advice is as follows.

1. Think carefully about your profile and link to your blog.

2. Join groups and follow topics that you are interested in.

3. Find questions where you can add value with your expertise and write helpful informative answers.

4. Link to your blog or website but be careful not to come across as too promotional.

5. Build relationships with other thought leaders in your field using some of the other techniques discussed in this book.

6. Use social media to share your content worthy of sharing.

Write for a publication or magazine

Did you ever have the dream where you walk into a newsagents or visit a newsstand, and you look at all the glossy magazines on the shelf? You find the one you are looking for and flick through the pages until you find it ... your article and picture staring back at you.

Well the good news is this isn't a pipe dream, it is totally achievable with the right strategies. I remember when my first magazine article was published, it was an in-flight magazine for a well-known airline, and for the whole month of September it would be on all of their flights.

I remember getting a call from my sister when she had been on a flight with her friends and one of them opened to the page and then shouted across the aisle 'Oh my god Mandy that's your brother!' That made her proud and me happy, it was a great feeling.

When it comes to writing, too many begin their journey the wrong way, in my opinion. They effectively try to start too big and become overwhelmed. They focus on the book contract, international fame and the speaking tour that comes with it.

In reality that's not quite how it all works. I have written this part of the book in this order (blogging, magazines then books) for a reason: because it is a natural progression with each stage making you a better writer and more attractive to the decision makers at the next stage.

Obviously, there is going to be some overlap in terms of benefits and strategy, so I am going to start with the benefits that specifically relate to writing for magazines.

Writing for magazines is a fantastic introduction to publishing
It will show you how it all works and give you the experience of what it's like to have your content edited. As a writer, you will develop your skills and learn what makes a topic desirable to the editor.

Writing for a magazine can help you reach your target market
Magazines typically have a focus or genre so can help you
identify and reach a specific audience. For example, if you are
a business person trying to raise your profile in the local area,
then a local magazine or newspaper supplement sounds like
an obvious choice. Maybe it's a specific industry you want to
target? Then there will be publications relating to that industry either through the associations and institutes or even
independent magazines. Or maybe it's a certain demographic
you want to reach, i.e. men, women, an ethnicity, a sexual persuasion, age etc. Well you guessed it, these publications
exist too.

Magazines typically have a longer life   Magazines tend to
endure more than simple press coverage like newspapers, and
in some cases they are even collectable. The interesting nature
of articles in a magazine can make them a semi-permanent
medium for exposure.

**Magazines almost always have a well-optimised, digital
version**   This of course means more results in search engines
when anyone Googles your name, as well as reaching new audiences by leveraging social media as most articles can be easily
shared.

Writing for a magazine can elevate your status   Many titles are
very well respected, so being published will increase your reputation using the principle of 'credibility by association'.

Magazines tend to have a more committed readership   In the
blogging section, I talked about the 'scan' nature of reading
online. With a magazine it is different; the reader may have paid
for their copy, the reading experience is more textural (including

the sense of touch) and the reader often will purposely set aside time to read.

You will build name recognition   Every reader, subscriber and advertiser will see your byline and start to get to know your work and style of writing. This can be really useful for getting a future book deal or other magazine opportunities or maybe even some speaking opportunities.

Getting published gives you confidence   I can tell you from personal experience, getting featured in a magazine gave me more confidence that a book could be a reality and motivated me to take my writing further.

Now the how

So, now we know why, we should take a look at how we go about it.

Well, like many things in life, it is more about who you know, not what you know. Building a relationship with an editor is the quickest and easiest way to find opportunities to contribute to their publication.

It is essential to realise that an editor plays a major part when it comes to producing quality work. Your ability to work with them to understand their objectives is essential when trying to identify what's required in the article.

An editor is the person responsible for bringing in new content which will be read, appreciated and hopefully shared. Editors work to tight deadlines and are inundated with requests for column inches. The easier we can make their jobs, the more likely it is that they will work with you now and in the future.

Now, we are going to assume you won't be rejected due to your content. Let's assume your story flows, your sentences are properly structured, grammar and spelling are correct and you haven't misused terminology. I hope we agree that these are basic requirements.

STEP 1: Do Your Research

In the first instance (and assuming you understand the type of audience you want to reach), you need to target a few publications that best suit your area of expertise. Once identified, start to read enough issues to familiarise yourself with the style and personality of the magazine. It is also a good idea to take this further by looking at their social channels, blogs and newsletters.

What is the average length of an article? What sort of headlines do they use?

Does their website share a list of upcoming themes and topics? If not then this is an ideal initial thing to request from the editorial team, along with submission guidelines, deadline dates etc.

STEP 2: Brainstorm Some Ideas

Based on your research and any upcoming themes, have an idea of how you can add value. Think about the topic and the angle you would take.

STEP 3: Build the Relationship with the Editor

Editors are human beings ;-) and I have often found picking up the phone to initially discuss your ideas or inviting them for a coffee a really good strategy. Caffeine is good when you are reading content all day.

STEP 4: Submit a Proposal

Now, it may be here that you need to write a proposal or query letter, which is a short, formal letter asking for consideration. Address them by name and include a short pitch for your idea. Better still . . . ideas . . . this will increase the likelihood of receiving a response.

When contacting an editor, it is always a good idea to include samples of your previous work, in the form of links if published online.

Most editors prefer a proposal before an article submission so they can discuss it with the writer and steer it down the right path. This is good news for you as it is more likely to be published. Whatever you do, listen to their advice!

STEP 5: Make Life Easy for Them

What time-poor, deadline-focused editorial teams really want is writers who make life easy for them. This means meeting deadlines. I know it is obvious, but if they have to chase you, it is unlikely they will use you again.

Provide a strong photograph which complements the article and fits with the publication's personality. Ensure the resolution is print quality. It is a tragedy when a great article is received, yet not published due to a lack of photo.

Deliver what was promised. Failure to stick to the proposal outline will frustrate an editor . . . they don't like surprises!

STEP 6: *Leverage Your Success*

Remember, this book is about building your influence. If you have a win with a publication, then make sure you let your network know by sharing through your social channels and maybe even blogging about it.

You could even create a section on your website called 'In the press' to impress your visitors and increase your credibility.

One final word about writing for magazines. It is very likely you will find yourself on the receiving end of a rejection letter. Expect this and don't give up.

Use a rejection as a learning experience and phone the editor up to find out where improvements could be made. Persistence is key! You could always send the article to another publication.

> *There are some more ideas about reaching editors and journalists later on in this chapter under the heading 'Using PR to Grow Your Influence'.*

A Moment of Reflection

- What publications would you like to write for?
- Check out their websites for editorial contact information.
- Create a few sample pieces if you don't already have them to show off what you can do.
- Create a one-page bio which clearly explains your experience and why you are qualified to be sharing thought leadership on this subject.

Remember, for the accompanying strategy template and other resources go to www.InfluenceTheBook.com.

Write a book

Publishing a book has many of the same advantages as writing a blog or for a magazine, so I won't repeat them. What I will do, though, is explain the unique benefits and overview your different publishing options.

Like I said right at the beginning of this book: I had to be convinced to do this, I had to be confident I had enough time to research, enough content for a book, enough space in my diary (capacity to get it done), enough confidence that I wouldn't be embarrassed with the end result.

At the time of writing this section I can tell you . . . it's really bloody hard work writing a book!

As a speaker, I know a lot of authors and therefore understand how a book has benefited them, which I will of course share. As the founder of a business community with tens of thousands of members, I can also tell you I have heard, on too many occasions to count, people say they have an idea and are going to write a book about it . . . and it never materialises. I now realise why . . . it's really bloody hard work writing a book!

You have to force yourself to sit down and focus, brainstorm ideas, research, write, edit, rewrite, research more, cut, edit, write, rewrite, more research, write etc. – I think you get the point – until you hit your target (normally north of 50,000 words). It is gruelling hard work and I suspect most people won't be able to do it.

In fact, research shows that over 85% of people in business would like to write a book yet only 5% actually do it!

While I am on the subject of the downsides, let me tell you some more. Knowing you are finished is almost impossible. Pretty much every section I have written so far I want to go back and edit, or add to it because I don't want to leave anything out for you or I am worried the content isn't strong enough. Let me tell you, these feelings are normal. It takes a badass to soldier through and eventually take the leap of faith and publish.

It is unlikely that writing a book will make you rich. I read recently that the average book sales figure is a mere 300 sales . . . 300 sales! And according to several publishers I spoke to, 3500 is considered acceptable for a business publication.

Have I put you off? I tried! I repeat: it's really bloody hard work writing a book!

That said, there are some fantastic upsides. Here are some of the very best.

Writing a book deepens your knowledge I kid you not, I thought I had enough knowledge and content before I even started the book, but through the ongoing research I have been exposed to more ideas, statistics and opinions which has given me a much deeper appreciation of the subject.

It creates an abundance of great content This content can be repurposed for speeches, blogs, magazines, white papers, tweets, LinkedIn articles and webinars etc. The process of writing a book really crystallises your thinking, bringing out your brightest and most important ideas.

It massively builds recognition, credibility and respect Adding the word 'author' to your title instantly gains you more respect and authority on your subject. This in turn makes you more attractive to the press and can give you almost celebrity status within certain environments, where everyone wants to speak to you.

It can help to advance your career   Yes, I realise many of you reading will already be the head honcho in your respective companies, but having a book could help you create non-executive directorships, positions on the board of your industry associations and trade institutes.

For those that aren't head honchos, publishing a book will gain you new respect from your employer and really cement your authority on your subject within your organisation.

It can be leveraged by your business   Imagine walking into your next business meeting with a copy of your new book instead of just a business card. As a general principle, wouldn't you be more likely to use the consultant that wrote the book on the subject? And following on from a previous chapter, when you gift knowledge you create that deep desire to reciprocate.

Many people I know have increased both their volume of work and their fee simply by being published. So if the book never made a fortune in book sales, it certainly can increase your fees.

Also, you may be able to leverage your book to run seminars or workshops relating to it. Maybe this is possible to licence so other people can deliver your training. You could also write the keynote presentation which pays a speaker fee but opens you up to bigger audiences, who in turn might need all of the above. Think about it . . . this means the simple act of being an author could help you attract more pre-qualified prospects, which allows you to raise your rates and be **PICKY** as to who you want to work with.

Writing a book makes you a better writer and editor   The skill-set you develop whilst producing a book helps you improve your writing across the other areas of your business, i.e. marketing literature, proposals, emails, speeches, blog etc., and you will even improve the way you organise and articulate your ideas and thoughts.

I have found that I have become better at self-editing (although I do this at a different time because there is a difference between using the creative side of your brain and the auditing side that requires attention to detail). I have become more disciplined not only with the writing of the book but with other projects within the business.

From a content creation point of view, you will become more curious. About everything! Whilst being open to new ideas you will also become more analytical and critical in your thinking.

It is pure marketing magnetism   Think of all those additional pages which will be found when someone Googles your name. Not just on your website of course, but on Amazon too. Even when you sign off your blog posts you can reference your book to give your blog even more credence.

The average business person might come up against obstacles when seeking media attention or publicity, mainly because they may be perceived as simply seeking free advertising. As the published authority on the subject, you are sought out for expert opinion or your book is reviewed, which is kind to your marketing budget.

And lastly, writing a book increases your confidence   It's a great sense of achievement holding your first book in your hands – remember only 5% of people that want to write actually follow through. Your book is evidence that you know how to focus and complete a project.

Your publishing options

So, maybe you listened more to just how bloody hard it is to write a book and I put you off, or you are made of stronger stuff and got excited by the benefits and I inspired you to take action. If the latter is true, you will be interested in your options when it comes to publishing.

Authors now have a choice in how they publish and get their books into the hands of readers. I am only going to discuss the merits of traditional publishing and self-publishing, although there are variations on the respective themes.

It is also worth noting that many authors use both forms of publishing depending on the project, hopefully this will help you evaluate your options.

Traditional Publishing

Traditional publishing is essentially the established process of getting a book deal, which involves submitting your book to an agent or the publisher direct, and hopefully results in a contract.

The Pros

Prestige and Credibility   Getting your book idea past the gate-keepers in a publishing company is usually validation that your work is up to scratch. This increases your credibility as an author and, rightly or wrongly, many will take you more seriously.

Better Distribution   This in my opinion is one of the key benefits of working with a major publisher and totally what they are geared up to do. Publishers have more clout with retailers and distributers, and are supported by reps who in turn visit stores trying to make it as easy as possible to sell their titles.

Retailers like it because they take inventory on sale or return with a single invoice.

You have a much bigger chance of featuring in a major book store through a traditional publishing deal.

More Support   Working with a traditional publisher means you have access to a team of professionals whose job it is to get the best out of you. From editors to cover designers, from formatting to marketing, an experienced team is provided as part of the contract.

This really suits authors who just want to produce content.

No Upfront Fees   In fact, often there is a cash advance against future royalties. If you are asked for upfront fees then it won't be a traditional publisher, more likely a vanity publisher.

Remember, it is an advance on royalties. Whatever your agreed rates, your book will need to pay back the advance before you earn any more money from it.

More Likely to Lead to Other Opportunities   Because of the kudos of working with a traditional publisher, you are more likely to get PR opportunities on the back of your book and other media/TV-related work.

The Cons

It Can Be a Slow Process   If you have to find an agent, who in turn finds a publisher, you may find the process can take 6–18 months, if not longer. The writing and editing will be the same regardless of your publishing preference.

Less Creative and Editorial control   You essentially give this up when you sign the contract. I know many authors that haven't been happy with their titles, marketing strategies and cover designs. It's even worse if you disagree with your editor.

This is why it helps to have a clear vision of your book concept when negotiating, and cultivate strong relationships with your team.

Lower Royalties   Royalties are a percentage of the book sale price, usually between 6 and 25 percent, and are likely to be net – which means calculation after discounts, returns and overheads. The percentage you command will be down to several factors, including your track record (more risk with first-time authors) and the market demand for your topic.

If you have gone through an agent, you could also be sharing your royalties whether they have sold the work or not. Read the small print.

Remember, it's a business and your publisher is looking for a return on their investment. Their industry works because they understand how to reduce their risks.

Royalties are also paid twice a year!

Harder to Break Into   As above, it's a business which is risk adverse. First time authors can improve their chances of a traditional publishing deal by demonstrating they already have an audience and ideas for promotion.

Increasingly authors have to do their own marketing as the publisher's marketing focus is usually concentrated on retailers, not consumers. If you do want a traditional deal, maybe make this part of your negotiation.

So should you take a traditional publishing deal? Absolutely you should. For the right project and the right contractual terms. Only you will know what suits you after you have evaluated both the pros and cons.

I have chosen to publish this book with Capstone because I am confident they have bought into my vision for the book, and I know the weight of a top publisher will afford me many benefits I may have struggled to achieve on my own.

Self-Publishing

A self-publishing author is often referred to as being an 'indie author' (independent) and, for some, this conjures an image of someone doing everything themselves, primarily as a hobby. This is not true. I know many authors who have chosen this route because they can drive sales themselves and choose to make more margin.

The Pros

Total Creative Control   Both of the content and the design. This is a common appeal for authors who have clashed with traditional publishers in the past. They simply work with the freelancers of their choice for designs.

Additionally, you have the flexibility to change the cover or retitle your book, maybe even create an updated edition. All in your control.

Better Payment Terms   This is both from higher commissions and better regularity with monthly payments. This means you don't have to sell as many books to achieve the same revenues. I would caution though: remember it is influence we are trying to grow; fewer sales won't necessarily achieve this.

Quicker Turnaround   As I said, the writing and editing is the same for both options but an indie author can get their eBook title selling in as little as four hours from uploading to Amazon, iBooks, Kobo etc.

It Can Be Better for a Niche   Remember, traditional publishers are in it for a return, so if you are trying to create more influence in a niche then you might not be an attractive proposition for them. Self-publishing certainly helps you overcome this problem.

Self-publishing Can Lead to Better Traditional Publishing Deals   If you prove yourself first by going it alone, you are in a much stronger position when it comes to negotiating your next book contract.

The Cons

It Can Be a Lonely Old Process   Not only does it fall on you to do the writing and marketing, but you may also find yourself editing (not advised), formatting and designing the cover, subject to your budget. You may not have the time or confidence to do it alone.

More Likely to Cost You Up Front   If you are going to outsource design and editing etc., then it will cost you. If you don't have a budget, then the traditional route starts to look more attractive.

Less Kudos   This is a con that is getting smaller every day. In fact, the most likely people to judge you are agents and publishers.

Fewer sales   Well, for a start, it is harder to get print distribution with offline retailers although not impossible . . . it is just one more job you will be doing yourself.

As I mentioned above, there are alternatives out there, but I would encourage you to do your due diligence before you part with any cash. Make sure you speak with their other authors and get testimonials before you decide and you won't go too far wrong.

A Moment of Reflection

- If you were to write a book, what would it be about?
- What would the main lessons be for the reader?
- What books in this genre do you already admire? Which were successful?
- What are you doing differently?

Remember, for the accompanying strategy template and other resources go to www.InfluenceTheBook.com.

INFLUENCE BY PUBLIC SPEAKING

Speaking from a podium or presenting can be a really powerful way to raise your profile and become an authority. **Make sure you join the Facebook group Speakers Corner which has over 8,000 members from around the world.**

> *'Speech is power: speech is to persuade, to convert, to compel.'*
>
> **Ralph Waldo Emerson**

Now, I feel you cringe immediately as the memories come flooding back of your school days when you were forced to stand and speak in front of your classmates and how nervous you felt.

Of course, you are not alone with this anxiety. Of all of the fears out there, fear of public speaking is said to affect 75% of us, making it number one in the league of fear. LOL. Reading that back it sounds like a really crummy comic book title *The League of Fear*. It amuses me that fear of death comes second.

Anyway, if that is true, and so many are scared to do it, that surely means it's not a common strategy? More importantly, it may be an opportunity for you to stand out.

Yes, sure, it means overcoming your fear, but trust me, you get used to it very quickly and there are many gentle introductions to get you started. As an international public speaker now, I can categorically assure you that my speaking has been the biggest vehicle for influence of all the strategies I use.

In this chapter I want to concentrate on three things. First, I will explain the benefits so you are left with no doubt that this is an important weapon in your armoury. Second, I will talk about how you might want to start creating your talks. Third, I will suggest some strategies for finding opportunities to speak.

You will note that this won't be a chapter on how to speak in public. There are many books on this topic as well as several professional organisations whose sole purpose is to support and develop speakers. I will reference these on my website *Influence TheBook.com*.

Benefits of Speaking

Personal Development   This is the obvious first benefit to stepping out of your comfort zone and taking the stage. There are several areas you will develop, as follows.

Improve Your Communication Skills   Actually, all areas of communication, not just your speaking. As a speaker, you will learn how to better structure your arguments, become more persuasive and be more definite in what you say. Your vocabulary will increase. Your listening will improve as you consider your audience and their feedback. Your reading will be honed as you look to research more to support your ideas. Lastly, and perhaps most importantly, you will become more aware of how you are being perceived by being a better reader of people.

Improve Your Critical Thinking   The process of writing a speech will strengthen your critical thinking, which in turn will make your arguments more robust.

Improve Your Confidence   Your self-image will change as you conquer your old self-doubt and anxiety. You will feel empowered and this will impact other areas of your life.

Improve Your Performance as a Speaker   I know it is obvious, but the more you speak the better you become at speaking. You will become more aware of timing, when to pause, improve your stage craft, become more articulate and learn to tell stories with varied tone and pace.

Personalise Your Brand   Speaking helps you achieve something that other marketing channels don't do as well. It lets you build instant rapport with your audience. A face-to-face, personal connection with a brand will beat a faceless interaction any day of the week. You and your brand will be remembered long after the event is over.

Accelerate the Growth of Your Network   You will of course be known by your audience in a far more powerful way than networking on its own can achieve. Better still, people will come to you as the authority. But it is much more than this: as a speaker you will rub shoulders with other speakers and influencers in your field. An ideal environment to create collaborative partnerships.

Build Your Authority   You will be perceived as an expert in your field and your reputation will grow. Sharing knowledge and adding value creates huge trust.

You Become a Leader   More than an authority, you become a leader when you share your message from the stage. By asking the right questions and presenting the right evidence you lead the thought processes of your audience and become a change agent. When something you said inspires change in others, it is incredibly satisfying.

Drive Traffic to Your Website   Many of your audience will look you up as a result of your talk. If you are clever, you will give them a reason to follow up with you, or let you with them. Simply making your slides available on your website or sharing a white paper after your talk is an excellent way to drive traffic, grow your social connections and keep the conversation going.

Impress your Boss   If you are an employee looking to climb the ladder, then confident public speaking is a great way to show leadership abilities. Your professionalism and poise will definitely put you in contention for promotion.

> *'Wise men speak because they have something to say; fools because they have to say something.'*
>
> **Plato**

Building Your Presentation

> *'I run on the roads, long before I dance under the lights.'*
>
> **Muhammad Ali**

This is one of my favourite quotes of all time and really sets the scene for a knockout presentation (see what I did there?). Preparation is everything!

What I want to do in this section is give you some ideas on how to structure your presentation to maximise impact. Having a structure really helps you stay on message and keep within your allotted time, there is nothing that will stress an event organiser more than a speaker seriously overrunning.

I am sure you have sat in many talks where the speaker appeared disorganised and rambling. It is highly likely that you found it hard to follow the presentation or learn any meaningful lessons.

You see, when a speech doesn't flow, an audience will quickly get lost. For the speaker, this is an opportunity missed!

There are several factors which will influence your choice of structure, but none more important than your overall goal. What is it you want to achieve? Are you trying to inspire your audience? Maybe the goal is to motivate them? Are you informing them on a topic or trying to persuade them with an argument? You may simply want to entertain?

Consider the needs of your audience   For example, their level of knowledge on your subject will dictate how much time you spend contextualising before reinforcing your main points. As you prepare the presentation, always keep in mind what the audience needs and wants to know, not what you can tell them. During your presentation, remain focused on your audience's response, and react to it. Make it easy for your audience to understand and respond.

Keep it Simple   Concentrate on your core message and always keep in mind the question: what is the key message for my audience to take away? Keep your core message focused and brief.

If what you are planning to say doesn't contribute to that core message, don't say it.

Open Strong   How you open your presentation is crucial. You need to grab attention and hold it. Your audience will give you a short period of grace in which to entertain them before they start to switch off, so don't waste it on explaining who you are. Try a story, a powerful quote or an attention-grabbing image.

Include your stories   We covered the power of story telling earlier in this book. It is essential for successful speaking. We have emotional reactions to stories, they help us focus, understand and remember. If you can use stories in your presentation, you will increase engagement and the retention of your message. As mentioned above, it is a good idea to start with a story, but even better if your whole presentation is a story.

Avoid Death by PowerPoint   Limit the number of slides you use; avoid small fonts and trying to cram too much on them. Better still, simply use big bold images instead so the audience is listening to your words and not reading them.
As a general rule, slides should be the sideshow to you, the speaker. Great slides should be useless without you. Remember, less is more . . . and keep it simple!
If you need to provide more information, drive them to your website and increase the chances of a relationship afterwards or ask for their business cards so you can email the information.

Call to Action   Include a call to action in your talk. Remember, if you are talking to demonstrate expertise and grow your influence, at the very least you want to continue the relationship.

Let your audience know how they can connect with you afterwards, and if you are making an offer or providing a follow-up, make sure your call to action is clear.

Practise Practise Practise   I cannot stress the importance of practising enough. Practising helps you deliver your killer lines naturally. It helps you appear cool, calm and collected. It helps you relax and focus on your audience. It helps you keep to your allotted time so as not to annoy the event organiser.

While delivering your talk

Don't talk down to your audience   The best speakers tap into the wisdom of the room and involve other influencers (credibility by association). So, instead of assuming you are the only one with something to say, open up the conversation so others can share their experiences as well.

Smile and Make Eye Contact   I mean with everyone. If you smile and make eye contact with your audience, you build rapport, which keeps them alert and listening to your content.

Show Your Passion   The most important thing is to connect with your audience, and the best way to do that is to let your passion for the subject show. Be enthusiastic and honest, and the audience will respond.

Use your Voice Effectively   We have covered tone of voice earlier in this book, but the spoken word is far more effective when you use your voice well.
Varying your pace, and emphasising changes in pitch and tone, will make your voice more interesting and keep your audience's attention.

Use your Body Effectively   As well as the tone of your voice, your body language is crucial to getting your message across. Avoid closed body language (a barrier to your audience) or fidgeting (distracting your audience) or pacing the stage.
Make your gestures open and confident, move naturally around the stage, and if possible, among the audience too.

Lastly Relax   Take a deep breath and enjoy the experience. Remember, they are there to learn from you. Take your time and don't rush.
If you can learn to relax, you will definitely deliver a more polished presentation. You will enjoy yourself more and so will your audience.

Finding Opportunities to Speak

Finally, on the subject of speaking, I want to give you some ideas on where to find the opportunities to speak in the first place.

To increase your chance of being booked, create a well-designed speaker bio (you can download mine from my website as an example). A good bio includes your contact details, your talk outline and what the audience will take away; some testimonials and, of course, an introduction to you and why you should be listened to.

Also, consider putting a showreel video together, preferably one which shows you in action with a couple of punchy soundbites. If there is an example of you talking to a larger audience, even better. Make sure it looks professional!

Business Networking Groups   Networking events take place every day all over the country, bringing local business owners together. Often the event format includes a speaker and this is a great place to start, and an ideal environment to practise. Networkers are more likely than anyone else to refer you on to other speaking opportunities.

Trade Associations   If your message is industry relevant, trade associations have numerous speaking opportunities – from annual conferences to regional meet-ups.
Identify the contact for events or education, send them your bio and showreel, then follow up. Associations are always looking for new talent to wow their members.

Business Publications and Magazines   Whether this is a local publication or a national magazine, most will contain an events listing. They may even organise their own events.

Your Suppliers and Customers   If they hold their own events there may be opportunities. They may also sponsor events where they can suggest or supply the speakers . . . ask!

Search Google   Seems obvious doesn't it? Try playing with different keywords to see what comes up. You can also set up alerts in the same way as you would for managing your online reputation.

Speaker Directories and Agencies   Speaker agencies work directly with event organisers to help find the right speaker for their events. They typically work on a percentage of your fee. There are a few free-to-register online directories which meeting planners sometimes go to which may help. Here are two to look at:
Speaker Services – speakerservices.com
Speaker Zone – speakerzone.com

Speaker Groups There are several not-for-profit membership organisations out there devoted to helping their members improve their speaking skills in a supportive environment.

> **Toastmasters International** – It also has its own speaking bureau.

> **Professional Speakers Association** – It also takes on associate members who are new to speaking.

Other Speakers Don't overlook other speakers in your network. Ask them where they speak, and for introductions where relevant. Better to collaborate with like-minded speakers and share opportunities. Together, you'll achieve so many more gigs! Also, look at the websites and LinkedIn profiles of competitors and other professionals who target your audience. Where have they spoken before?

Online Events Directories Each of these sites provides tools for people organising events around shared interests. Many will show you who is attending so you can sanity check that the audience is right for you. If in doubt, why not attend first?

- Meetup.com
- Eventbrite.com
- Facebook Events
- FindNetworkingEvents.com

Ask Your Audience Last but not least, while you're speaking, ask your audience. Pick an appropriate time (usually at the end, after you have bowled them over with your wit, charisma and humour . . . no pressure). You can say something like, 'Hopefully you can see I love my subject. If you know of an audience who might benefit from my talk, I would appreciate an introduction.' On my very first public talk I was lucky enough to pick up another three bookings. Don't underestimate this one!

A Moment of Reflection

- What topic do you want to speak on?
- What do you want the audience to feel as a result of your talk?
- What action do you want your audience to take?
- What are your unique qualities?
- Using your stories from the previous chapter, which of them best emphasise your message and can be used to structure your presentation?
- Take some time to identify potential events to speak at.
- Join the Speakers Corner group on Facebook for more useful advice and support.

Remember, for the accompanying strategy template and other resources go to www.InfluenceTheBook.com.

USING PR TO GROW YOUR INFLUENCE

> *'Some are born great, some achieve greatness and some hire public relations officers.'*
>
> **Daniel J. Boorstin**

The last area I want to touch on in this chapter on knowledge is public relations (PR). Now ordinarily I would put PR more in a marketing book, but there is a definite crossover for demonstrating expertise.

PR is one of the most cost-effective methods of raising brand awareness for you and your business. Coverage in relevant magazines, newspapers, websites or on TV helps develop you as a trusted authority within your niche.

If a simple tweet or positive comment can result in business, it stands to reason that there is much more credibility from a respected media brand. It might follow that their readership will share the article socially, amplifying your audience.

A good PR person will try to place thought leadership articles and expert interviews for their clients with a view to building their profile. If you can afford a good PR person, then go for it. Look for someone who is already doing this successfully for other individuals. If you can't afford a good PR person, then here are a few tips for you to get some good publicity.

Be Your News Source Create a page on your website where readers can see your latest news (written by you and featured in the press). Make it clear on this page how journalists can get in touch.

By having your own resource, you maintain more influence over the narrative you want to portray. Demonstrating your values and brand identity.

Create Amazing Content When creating an article or press release, focus on telling stories which are simple and concise. Think about the main point the reader should take away and make it clear.

Focus on the issues faced by readers, and present the solutions. Include examples of you doing this with your customers. Remember, keep it natural – more like a story than a sales pitch – and you increase the chances of getting published.

Be Honest When talking about yourself or your business, transparency is key. Always be honest and avoid exaggerating. Anything other than an authentic portrayal of your brand could be damaging.

Be Topical and Current To be trusted as a reliable source of information, you need to be up to date with the latest developments in your industry. You can do this with sources like Google Trends, social media, news, industry reports, forums, etc. Then produce relevant content on these topics. If you make this habitual, you'll have plenty of great ideas to pitch to editors, and you'll begin to see the results in your coverage.

Build Your Media Contacts You can start this one straight away. Build your database of editors and journalists both locally and nationally. Also consider your industry relevant publications.

Next, build relationships: introduce yourself and ask what they look for when considering articles to publish. One of the easiest things I did locally was to take the business editor of the regional newspaper to lunch. A relationship makes all the difference and you get to ask about upcoming features. Anything you can then do to make their life easier will be greatly appreciated.

Have a Presence Where Journalists Look   You need to make it as easy as possible for journalists to find you. Many journalists have mailing lists which they regularly consult. Request to be added.
The following sites will help you on your way with that.

- expertsources.co.uk
- sourcebottle.com
- responsesource.com
- journalism.co.uk
- helpareporter.com
- prnewswire.co.uk

Use Social Media   Social media is a great PR channel. It would be a mistake to focus all of your efforts on established media outlets only. Remember to be responsive – if someone gives negative feedback, respond immediately and politely. Avoid getting into drawn-out disputes online, move the conversation offline as soon as possible.

#journorequest   The hashtag #journorequest is used by journalists on Twitter looking for sources.

Consistency is Key   Success won't happen overnight. PR is a medium- to long-term strategy and consistency is key.

So, here endeth the section on knowledge, and how to get out there and demonstrate yours.

Remember, every day is a school day; and I will end on this quote:

> *'Never become so much of an expert that you stop gaining expertise. View life as a continuous learning experience.'*
>
> **Denis Waitley**

6

Y IS FOR YOU

The Qualities of Influencers

Over the last 48,000 words or so we have explored some of the practical and easy-to-implement strategies you can use to increase your influence. How you deal with people and form relationships, how you portray yourself both in person and online, how you communicate with others both in writing and speech, and lastly how you demonstrate knowledge and share your ideas.

So, to close this book I would like to share with you some of the personal qualities I most respect in effective influencers, and why. You may already have these qualities in abundance, but how well are they reflected in your actions and daily interactions with others?

Rather than wait until the end of the chapter before you reflect on what I am saying, let's do it as we go. But this time consider these three questions with regard to each quality as laid out below. And treat this as a serious exercise, not just you reading a book.

1. On a scale of 1–10: how much do you think you embody this particular quality?

2. On a scale of 1–10: if you were to ask all of your friends, family and colleagues how much they think you embody this quality, what do you think they would say?

3. For each of these qualities, what do you think you could do right away (make a list if you like) to embody them more and demonstrate them in your everyday interactions?

It is important for you to do this exercise with brutal honesty – if anything be harder on yourself. As another exercise, why not write your answers, then ask a friend, a family member and a colleague to share with you their score. Again, pick someone you know will give you a totally honest perspective.

If your scores match theirs, congratulations, you probably have really good self-awareness (which I will come on to), if there is a big difference, dig a little deeper and seek to understand why.

Just as a personal observation: I have always found a certain honesty from my detractors, which I hardly see from my supporters. Supporters, by definition, want to build you up, make you feel better, believe in what you do. Understand that this will skew their feedback.

So, in no particular order, let's get into it.

EFFECTIVE INFLUENCERS ARE AUTHENTIC

> 'But above all, in order to be, never try to seem.'
>
> **Albert Camus**

The simplest way I have heard authenticity described is 'When the voice inside your head says the same things as the voice outside you head.'

For me, I think, it is about not pretending to be something you are not, just being yourself. Whether that be in the words you write or the things you say, you don't hide behind a mask.

If you don't know the answer to something, you don't pretend. You allow others to see the traits that make you human and are not afraid to be vulnerable.

- Think about the way you interact with others. How authentic do you allow yourself to be?
- Think about someone you thought was inauthentic or hiding behind a mask in the past. How did you feel about them?

EFFECTIVE INFLUENCERS THINK ABOUT THE FUTURE

> *'I learn from thinking about the future, what hasn't been done yet. That's kind of my constant obsession.'*
>
> **John Cale**

Most of the influential people I know actually dedicate time to consider the future and can fairly accurately predict new trends within their industry or sphere of expertise.

They get involved. Involved in the industry events (speaking and organising), involved in thought leadership; and they are up to date with the ideas of other influencers too.

This gives them a phenomenal edge when it comes to change, they are usually a step ahead of it.

- When was the last time you thought about how your industry was changing?
- What do other influencers write or say about your industry?
- Does the future change in your industry present any opportunities?

EFFECTIVE INFLUENCERS LEVERAGE TECHNOLOGY

'The technology keeps moving forward, which makes it easier for the artists to tell their stories and paint the pictures they want.'

George Lucas

The most effective influencers have learnt to leverage technology. Whether it is using cloud and mobile platforms to get organised, or simply making collaboration easier.

They also reach new audiences through social media and spread thought leadership ideas through these channels.

- What sites are you not active on which could extend your reach?
- What technologies do your peers use to make their lives easier?
- Could you adopt them?

EFFECTIVE INFLUENCERS ARE COURAGEOUS

'Success is not final; failure is not fatal: it is the courage to continue that counts.'

Winston S. Churchill

Influencers, like leaders, have the courage of their convictions. They are willing to take calculated risks and pursue their goals without the fear of failure which holds so many people back. It takes courage to stand up and share what you believe and face the scrutiny and criticism of others.

They also accept that they need to step out of their comfort zones to stand on bigger stages and to increase their profile.

A great example of a leader showing courage is Matt Cutts, head of Google's Webspam team. Aside from being quite entertaining on Twitter, with over 500k followers, he is renowned for his sense of fairness. This was evidenced when he found out that Google had violated its own quality guidelines and, as a result, he took the decision to downgrade Google Chrome's homepage. Now *that* took courage.

- Where are you playing it safe right now?
- What from this book do you consider outside of your comfort zone?
- What can you do right now to push a personal boundary?

EFFECTIVE INFLUENCERS ARE GREAT COMMUNICATORS

> 'Communication – the human connection – is the key to personal and career success.'
>
> **Paul J. Meyer**

I have dedicated a lot of this book to communication, so it is no surprise I think it is an essential quality for creating influence.

Influence is all about sharing ideas and making them stick, and most influential communicators utilise multiple channels. They speak on stages or on camera, write for themselves and for others and are great one-to-one.

Influential people understand that in order to keep a project on track, you need to regularly maintain contact with all stakeholders to ensure everyone is getting the support they need and is on target.

- When you review the previous chapters, in what areas are you strong?
- Again, from these chapters, where could you improve?
- What opportunities do you have at your disposal to practise in these areas?

EFFECTIVE INFLUENCERS HAVE INTEGRITY

> 'Integrity is doing the right thing, even if nobody is watching.'
>
> **Jim Stovall**

Integrity is the congruence between what you know, what you claim, and the actions you take – and the best influencers have it in spades.

They disclose potential conflicts of interest, work transparently, value honesty and simply do the right thing. Their values shine through in every interaction and they have a reputation for being ethical.

- Who do you respect in business that you feel matches these traits?
- Can you remember a time when you didn't act with integrity? How did you feel?
- Can you remember a time when you know you did the right thing? How did you feel?

EFFECTIVE INFLUENCERS SHOW HUMILITY

> *'True humility is not thinking less of yourself; it is thinking of yourself less.'*
>
> **C.S. Lewis**

Humility is being open to the fact you could be wrong about something and don't necessarily know all of the answers.

It is having the confidence and self-awareness to recognise the talents of others, without being threatened by them. It is about nurturing and encouraging.

The most influential people I know contain their egos. They stay grounded and create an environment conducive to critical feedback . . . and they listen to it. Basically, they reside in reality!

- Who in your network keeps you grounded?
- How self-aware are you? Remember to take the test on my website.
- List your strengths and weaknesses and identify areas for development.

EFFECTIVE INFLUENCERS ARE FOCUSED

> *'The man who chases two rabbits, catches neither.'*
>
> **Confucius**

Influencers rarely spread themselves too thin. They don't try and build their influence in more than one industry, although there are exceptions.

They complete projects because they don't take too many on at any one time. This means they get a reputation for getting the job done.

A client of mine employs about 60 staff in his accountancy firm, but is also an author, speaker and soon-to-be TV personality. He told me that when he tries to write at work, he can't concentrate due to constant interruptions. At home his kids want his attention. So, he creates the conditions where he can focus by booking long train trips where there is nothing to do but write.

- What are you working on right now?
- How many balls are you juggling?
- Could you park one or two things while you focus on one project as a result of something you have read in this book?

EFFECTIVE INFLUENCERS ARE PREPARED

> *'Fortune favours the prepared mind.'*
>
> **Louis Pasteur**

Actually, influencers are organised in general. This is definitely an ongoing area of much-needed improvement for me; but I believe it is the difference between those that want to be influential and those that actually are.

Influencers tend not to 'wing it', they research thoroughly before they publish and they prepare well before important meetings.

They are also productive on the move, making calls in the car or writing on the train. They value their own time and know how to use it to the fullest extent.

- What tasks do you automate using technology tools?
- Where do you lack organisation?
- How could you utilise your travel time?

EFFECTIVE INFLUENCERS ARE CONFIDENT

> *'Believe you can and you're halfway there.'*
>
> **Theodore Roosevelt**

Influencers have enormous self-belief, which enables them to stand on any platform really confident in their convictions. Because they believe what they say, so does their audience.

Remember, the team around you looks to you when things go wrong. So it is up to you to remain calm and confident so that these qualities trickle down to them.

- In what area of your work do you lack confidence?
- And what is the reason for that?
- What can you do about it? List some ideas.

EFFECTIVE INFLUENCERS ARE INSPIRATIONAL

> *'If your actions inspire others to dream more, learn more, do more and become more, you are a leader.'*
>
> **John Quincy Adams**

Being able to inspire is essential if you want to influence people or effect change. Being inspirational uses a combination of many of the other qualities I mention in this section – connecting on an emotional level to share a vision for change, or simply to motivate.

Many influencers set an example and model behaviours which inspire others to take action. Akio Toyoda is an excellent example of this when he took over as CEO of Toyota in 2009. Not content with sitting in his ivory tower, he became personally invested in product excellence, even getting behind the wheel to test drive new models.

- Who do you consider inspirational in your network?
- What are the traits that make them inspirational?
- What can you do to model their behaviours?

EFFECTIVE INFLUENCERS ARE PASSIONATE

> *'People with passion can change the world.'*
>
> **Steve Jobs**

Every influencer I can think of has immense enthusiasm for their work or cause. People are drawn towards them because their passion is infectious. This passion makes all the difference.

Consider this. Imagine a member of staff who is highly educated, with the right aptitude and experience for the job, but has no interest. Their heart just isn't in it. Now consider the alternative, the less-educated member of staff who loves what they do and volunteers for everything. I know which one I would rather have in my team.

It's the passionate people that drive organisations forward. Be one of them.

- Think of the most passionate leaders you know. How does their passion show?
- Reflect on your last ten interactions with customers, your boss, your colleagues or your network. How passionate were you?
- What could you have done to demonstrate your enthusiasm more?

EFFECTIVE INFLUENCERS ARE RESILIENT

> *'They tried to bury me, but didn't know that I'm a seed.'*
>
> **Mexican proverb**

Resilience is vital for success in today's sometimes brutal working environment. It is easily defined as the ability to recover quickly from setbacks or the toughness to get back on the horse after a fall.

We all face difficulties throughout our careers, and it is natural to dwell sometimes on what went wrong, or compare ourselves to others, which further amplifies the negative emotional spiral. But resilient people don't stay there very long, instead they learn the lesson quickly and dust themselves off.

Your ideas, once shared, will face criticism from time to time; don't take it personally, seek the truth in what people say and stay resilient.

- Think back to a time when things didn't go to plan. How did you handle it?
- What would you do differently now?

EFFECTIVE INFLUENCERS ARE CONNECTED

> *'Everything you want in life is a relationship away.'*
>
> **Idowu Koyenikan**

Influencers prioritise people over everything else. They play an active part in their networks, fully engaged with other influencers, creating opportunities to collaborate and mutually support.

Influencers recognise that it is the depth of a relationship that counts, and that it is easier to influence people who trust you, than it is complete strangers.

- How would you honestly rate your network?
- If you were to wave a magic wand right now and add five new people to your network, who you could build a meaningful relationship with, who would they be?
- What steps could you take straight away to make this happen?

EFFECTIVE INFLUENCERS ARE DECISIVE

> *'We all make choices, but in the end our choices make us.'*
>
> **Ken Levine**

For me, it isn't just about making the decision, it is also being in a position to influence the outcome when the decision isn't yours to make.

Leaders are often called upon to make the big decisions, and being decisive inspires confidence in those around you. Influencers don't suffer from analysis paralysis; of course I am not saying that they don't consider carefully the potential outcomes, but they are prepared to make the call and take responsibility.

- Reflect on the last three big decisions you had to make. How long did it take you?
- What would have made you comfortable enough to come to a quicker decision?

EFFECTIVE INFLUENCERS ADAPT

> 'It is not the strongest of the species that survives, nor the most intelligent; it is the one most adaptable to change.'
>
> **Charles Darwin**

Influencers recognise that in order to stay relevant they need to adopt new approaches and utilise new technologies. They understand that whilst their message may be constant, everything else evolves.

In an ever-changing world, having the ability to adapt your thinking in response to the change around you makes you a much sought after thought leader.

Influencers ask different questions, take on multiple perspectives, consider the big picture and experiment.

- How fixed are you in your thinking?
- When did you last visit your message, and hold it up against the change around you?

EFFECTIVE INFLUENCERS ARE CHARISMATIC

> 'The reason we're successful, darling? My overall charisma, of course.'
>
> **Freddie Mercury**

We are all seduced by charisma. Influential people are naturally charismatic, arguably because they demonstrate the other qualities in this book.

Charisma helps you get attention, it draws people in. Think of a charismatic person you know and what happens when they walk into a room. An influencer knows how to use their charisma; they work the room and their energy is contagious.

When a charismatic person speaks with you, it makes you feel important, they actively listen to your words and give you their full attention in that moment.

- What can you do to increase your charisma? Maybe manage your energy better, sharpen your image, smile and increase your self-belief for starters?
- Reflecting on the charismatic people you know, what makes them stand out to you?
- How can you replicate their behaviour so it is right for you?

EFFECTIVE INFLUENCERS ARE GENEROUS

> *'Generosity is the most natural outward expression of an inner attitude of compassion and loving-kindness.'*
>
> **Dalai Lama XIV**

Kindness is often confused with weakness, and mistakenly so. Being generous with your time and the consideration you show others goes a long way towards winning fans.

Influencers are generous also with their content, sharing ideas and willing to help others develop their knowledge. They are not threatened by this.

They are also generous with their praise and prefer to build people up.

- What do you consider the benefits of generosity?
- Who in your environment could you help more right now?
- What could you incorporate into your everyday life to foster more generosity?

EFFECTIVE INFLUENCERS HAVE GOOD INTUITION

'You must train your intuition – you must trust the small voice inside you which tells you exactly what to say, what to decide.'

Ingrid Bergman

Intuition sits between instinct and reason. It is the bridge that joins the conscious and unconscious parts of our mind, and gives us the ability to know or feel something without analytical reasoning.

You will have heard the expressions 'trusting your gut' or 'having a hunch' before, and I am sure made decisions ignoring your gut . . . and regretted it.

Great influencers incorporate intuition into their decision making, they draw upon their experience, their knowledge, their logic *and* the way they feel about the decision. They also use their intuition with people to understand how they feel and think, which helps when developing relationships.

- Think back to a time when you went against your gut. What was the outcome and how did you feel about it afterwards?
- Now do the opposite, think when your gut has served you well because you listened to it.

EFFECTIVE INFLUENCERS ARE PERSISTENT

> *'Ambition is the path to success; persistence is the vehicle you arrive in.'*
>
> **William Eardley IV**

Persistence is right up there as one of the qualities we admire the most. It is the determination to complete a task despite setbacks, obstacles and naysayers.

You will have heard the phrase 'When the going gets tough, the tough gets going', which I believe applies perfectly to the persistent entrepreneur. They don't let fear or doubt paralyse them or cloud their judgement, and they have an unwavering commitment to their vision.

The persistent earn our respect and are more likely to succeed, which naturally increases their influence.

EFFECTIVE INFLUENCERS ARE DISCIPLINED

> *'Discipline is the bridge between goals and accomplishment.'*
>
> **Jim Rohn**

All of your planning will go to waste if you aren't self-disciplined and able to form good habits. It is so easy to be distracted in a digital age with so much stimulation and opportunity around us.

In business, there are already enough people who don't deliver on time, who arrive at meetings late and don't hit their targets. Don't be one of them. Being disciplined, turning up on time, meeting your obligations, hitting your deadlines and generally being consistent and reliable will make you stand out from the crowd.

- What tools do you use to keep focused on the task in hand?
- What routines or habits do you have to keep you on track?

EFFECTIVE INFLUENCERS ARE ACCOUNTABLE

> *'It is wrong and immoral to seek to escape the consequences of one's acts.'*
>
> **Mahatma Gandhi**

Personal accountability is taking responsibility for your actions, owning your mistakes and seeking solutions. In leadership, it will earn you trust and respect from your colleagues and customers, because they know you will keep your word.

Being accountable to others – your mentor, mastermind group other members of your board – is a great way to keep you focused. If you lack these people in your work place you may want to seek them out.

- Here is a question for you: why would you trust someone with no accountability?
- Who in your life holds you accountable? How do they do it?
- How do you hold yourself to account?

EFFECTIVE INFLUENCERS ARE VISIONARIES

> 'Be brave enough to live the life of your dreams according to your vision and purpose instead of the expectations and opinions of others.'
>
> **Roy Bennett**

Being visionary means being able to create a shared sense of purpose, and then to communicate it effectively to others so they want to be part of it.

Let's face it, change is uncomfortable, an effective influencer will share a vision appealing to both hearts and minds and motivate others to work towards it.

- Think about your vision for your future. Can you describe it easily?
- Think about your vision for your industry. What would need to happen for it to become a reality?
- Who needs to share in your vision to ensure its success?

EFFECTIVE INFLUENCERS ARE POSITIVE

> *'Surround yourself with positive people and you'll be a positive person.'*
>
> **Kellie Pickler**

Being positive gives you an energy. It's magnetic, drawing people in and making you more attractive. What's more, it's infectious.

Positivity has health benefits too, by reducing your negative self-talk you in turn reduce your stress levels. Relaxed and calm people inspire confidence.

Research suggests that positive thinkers have a greater capacity to take on new information, increasing their ability to connect the dots and see the bigger picture. And this can help you make better decisions.

- How do you act under pressure and how does this impact your relationships?
- How do you demonstrate positivity in your communications?
- Think back on your last five customer interactions. How could you have made them more positive and what do you think the benefits of this could be?

EFFECTIVE INFLUENCERS ARE GREAT WITH OTHER PEOPLE

> *'Beginning today, treat everyone you meet as if they were going to be dead by midnight. Extend them all the care, kindness and understanding you can muster. Your life will never be the same again.'*
>
> **Og Mandino**

Most influencers have the natural ability to disarm others, making them feel less guarded and special. They are masters of small talk and show genuine interest in other people, whether it be at a conference, a customer meeting or even on social media.

They are unafraid to pay a sincere compliment and know the power they can wield, when they are appropriate of course.

- When interacting with others, how much do you think about how they are feeling?
- Think about the last time someone paid you a compliment in a business setting. How did it make you feel?
- How could you make a small change to your communication to incorporate this trait?

EFFECTIVE INFLUENCERS ARE OPEN MINDED

> *'A mind is like a parachute. It doesn't work if it is not open.'*
>
> **Frank Zappa**

Some people approach every situation with an open mind but, sadly, for most it is a real challenge. Influencers do it naturally, understanding that by thinking openly they embrace new ideas. Because they demonstrate an open mind, others are more likely to share their insights with them and this in turn creates an environment for opportunity.

Becoming more open minded is as simple as:

1. Listening better.
2. Avoiding snap decisions by seeking all information first.
3. Showing appreciation for others' input.
4. Encouraging robust discussion.

   - Think of the last time one of your ideas was challenged. How did you react?
   - How could you have handled the situation better?

EFFECTIVE INFLUENCERS RECIPROCATE

> 'To be a best friend, the best word to live by is reciprocity.'
>
> **Debasish Mridha**

Anyone who truly understands influence, knows the power of reciprocation. When someone scratches their back, they are the first to scratch back; and they understand the subconscious, deep rooted desire to return favours.

- Think about every strong relationship you have, what is the value exchange? In other words, what do you get from the relationship and what do they get? When it is one sided it rarely lasts very long.
- Who has recently gone out of their way for you? Do you feel a desire to return the favour?

EFFECTIVE INFLUENCERS UNDERSTAND EVERYTHING IN THIS BOOK

'Good intentions are a waste of time without action and implementation.'

Warren Cass

I really hope you have taken several actionable ideas from the preceding pages and that it starts to make a difference to your goals.

I would really like to know the parts in particular that motivated a change and, once applied, produced results. Please let me know via @WarrenCass on Twitter.

Remember, this is just the start. Whatever your numbers were for the traits of influence above, they can be improved. Revisit this last chapter again regularly and reassess yourself. Thank you for reading.

INDEX

Printed and bound by CPI Group (UK) Ltd, Croydon, CR0 4YY